BAD
CHOICES
MAKE
GOOD
STORIES

My Life with Autism

DYLAN 'DIELAWN' VOLK

The Sequel to *Chasing the Rabbit*

Softcover ISBN: 978-1-7327179-0-9
Ebook ISBN: 978-1-7327179-1-6

Published by:
D & A Publishing, LLC
11 Morin St., Biddeford, ME 04005
www.chasingtherabbit.org

Produced by:
Grace Peirce
Great Life Press
www.greatlifepress.com

Cover design: Daniel Yeager

Library of Congress Control Number: 2018957794

Author's website: www.badchoicesmakegoodstories.com

To my dedicated mother, Amy,
who has stuck with me through the fire,
to the limit, to the wall

John!

Enjoy this book

Contents

Foreword

I met Dielawn in 2017. I'm not sure if you know this about him, but he has a tendency to say what's on his mind regardless of the social repercussions. Often it is because he doesn't know the social repercussions, so he says what he's thinking and people sometimes get angry.

One of the most significant things Dielawn has ever said to me is about honesty. He said, "People always say 'honesty is the best policy' but it's not true. When you actually tell the truth, people get really mad at you." This was stated in a moment of frustration, but it's so true.

Now back to when I met Dielawn.

For the first seven months of 2017, I was taking care of a homeless guy. He lived with me, he went everywhere with me, and he interacted with all of the people I interacted with. This homeless guy was with me when I met Dielawn.

We were out with a bunch of friends at a bar in Koreatown in Los Angeles, and he came over to the table where I was sitting and joined right into the conversation. Soon after he got to the table, Dielawn—as I mentioned before—said what was on his mind regardless of the social repercussions. Right away, the homeless guy who was with me started yelling at Dielawn. Full-on yelling. The others guys at the table got silent, Dielawn got silent, and I got silent.

Dielawn and I still reminisce about that day.

Now, when Dielawn and I hang out, we talk a lot about what people say versus what they expect socially. I know he's learning a lot about feelings and emotions and social honesty from hanging out with me, and I know I'm learning a lot about being authentic from Dielawn.

—Jeffrey Mark Klein

Introduction

In the making of this book, I took a microphone and told the story of my entire life from around age sixteen on. After several weeks we had a lot of material to work with, and I was faced with the process of having to choose what to keep and what to leave out. It reminded me a lot of trying to take notes in high school, where you were supposed to know what information was important, and what information wasn't. I have always struggled to sift information in that way—I felt like all the material was important! And especially with this being my life I'm sharing with you, I guess you could say I had a very egalitarian stance toward my stories and said, "They're all equal!" I needed help narrowing my stories down so I asked a few smart people for advice. They suggested that for every story I should be thinking, what is the point of this story? I needed to consider what the reader would take away from it, particularly if they have a child or know someone on the spectrum. This was still a painstaking process because to me, ALL my stories had a point. They provide a window into my life, which is consumed by autism, even when it doesn't seem like it to the outsider. Not to mention, you can decide for yourself after reading this, but I tend to think I'm a pretty interesting guy . . . very few boring things have ever happened to me. So what you've got here is not going to be everything I wanted to tell you. There was so much juicy content left on the cutting room floor just because I didn't want to put out a book the size of the Qur'an. The good news is, if you like what you see here, there's plenty more where these stories came from! And I can tell you that the ones left out are all important to me, so that means there is someone out there with autism, or a parent, educator, or counselor who would relate to and benefit from every story I have to tell. So here's what I need you to do—

Follow me on social media, I'm @RealDielawn everywhere: YouTube, Facebook, Twitter, Instagram, Snapchat, let's be friends!

Go to BadChoicesMakeGoodStories.com to get the scoop on bonus chapters, upcoming webinars, speaking engagements, and social media discussions that will be focused on chapters in the book, the chapters left out, and my life since the book was released.

I have a feeling once you get through this you'll be craving more, like the book version of salt and vinegar chips.

Is There a "Normal"?

The first book I wrote (with my dad) was *Chasing the Rabbit: A Dad's Life Raising a Son on the Spectrum.* My dad chose that title—he always describes me with the analogy of a greyhound chasing a mechanical rabbit: the greyhound can see the rabbit but can never catch it.

My dad says that the rabbit represents normal, and I'm the greyhound.

As someone with Asperger's—what's now called "high-functioning autism"—I am always trying to be "normal." I know what "normal" is, and I know what "normal" looks like, but I am perpetually trying to catch the rabbit, which is "normality." A lot of people have an issue with the term "normal." I don't. When people say things like, "There's no such thing as normal," it devalues the struggle I go through every day.

I can tell you, from twenty-seven years of living on the autism spectrum, that there is such a thing as normal. And it's okay to want to be normal. It's okay to aspire to be normal. And to all the normies reading this, you're okay just the way you are! Let me elaborate—at eight years old, if I had been obsessed with scoring the winning soccer goal for my team that would have been normal. When I was eight years old, I was obsessed with leaving church early on Sunday morning so I could write down the number one song on Kasey Kasem's American Top 40. That was not normal! There's nothing wrong with admitting that. I always knew it was true, so I found it very frustrating when people would say, "There's no such thing as normal." *Yes, there is.*

When I was in high school, I attended a seminar at Northeastern University for people with Asperger's. There was another individual there (pretty safe bet he was on the spectrum) who raised his hand and repeated the cliché "there's no normal." He said, "We're all different! We're all weird in our own way! So, there really is no such thing as normal."

I raised my hand and said, "You know what? That's *bullsh*t.* There *is* such a thing as normal! The difference between us and everybody else is that they all have quirks that fall within the range of what society considers normal, and we fall outside that range." I almost felt bad, because he didn't have much to say after that.

On the way back to the car, my dad said, "Where did you come up with that? That was really profound!" I said, "Dad, I have probably a hundred profound thoughts like that every day. I just happened to say that one!" And that was real talk. Let me assure you, if you like profound thoughts, you're going to like this book.

Anyway, if you know someone on the spectrum, it is okay to acknowledge that they're not "normal." It may come as a relief for them to admit that their brain function means they are not typical. It doesn't take anything away from who I am or my worth as a person. It's just a fact of life that those of us with autism live with every day.

For the longest time, I didn't like to acknowledge my disability. I would get angry at my parents' use of the word "Asperger's" (now called "high-functioning autism" or "autism spectrum disorder"). I would ask them not to even use the word. I hated the word "Asperger's." I mean, who came up with that name? I guess having no social skills isn't embarrassing enough.

I did not realize it at the time, but I think I was actually reacting that way for a very intelligent reason. I knew instinctively that the rest of the world did not view me as disabled, so it wasn't doing me any good to view myself that way. I think I was trying to set my mind to meet the standards I knew were going to be placed on me whether I liked it or not. They might have been standards I couldn't reach, but I knew I better get used to trying. I wish I could have articulated that when I was fourteen or fifteen. My parents and teachers simply saw me as rebellious and having a bratty attitude. And while I certainly did have a bratty attitude, this was me trying to prepare myself for a world that didn't give a sh*t about my autism.

I encourage you to read our first book, *Chasing the Rabbit*, because it will give you a very different perspective on my life, as it is mostly from my dad's point of view. This book is about all the ways that I, and millions of people with autism, experience the world. If you liked the "Dylan's Takes" from *Chasing the Rabbit*, you will love this book.

Welcome to my world!

Save The Best for First

It is ironic that sometimes what comes first in life is not at all representative of what lies on the road ahead. For a couple of years beginning when I was five, I had a friend named Jack who lived a few houses down. Jack was a very normal kid; we were in the same class in school and hung out almost every day. There was another kid who lived across the street who sometimes hung out with us, but to me, it felt like Jack and I were best friends.

Jack and I liked the same things. In 1997, this meant watching *Star Wars* every day and finding cool sticks in the woods. We got along, and I don't really remember anything other than a pretty typical friendship between kindergarten boys. It was nice to start my childhood off having a best bud that lived a few doors away, because nothing like that ever happened again. This was the first of several times in life I found out the hard way that your very first *(insert anything)* can sometimes end up as a cruel reminder of how rare it really is. It's an interesting phenomenon, there should really be a word for it!

Fast-forward to fall 1998: my parents decided to move our family from Portland to Sedgefield, a burgeoning suburb. Our new neighborhood had no shortage of boys my age, and they would get together every day after school and play street hockey right across the street from our house. They'd play for hours and hours, barely speaking at all. It turned out every kid in our entire neighborhood pretty much had Asperger's syndrome for hockey.

I tried over and over again to fit in with these guys and even got out there and played hockey with them. But no matter what I did, the neighborhood kids wouldn't include me in their group. I would see them outside every day playing together, riding their bikes together right past my house, but never knocking on my door. Instead, my mom would get word from one of their moms that they were all playing video games, and "Dylan is welcome to come over."

My mom would encourage me to join them. She wanted me to have a normal social life just as much as I did. I knew I belonged there, that these regular, cookie cutter kids were not too good to hang out with me. I have never had an issue with being assertive, so I would go right over and claim my spot.

The other moms were always welcoming and exceptionally friendly. They would often advocate for me, urging their sons, "Why don't you boys ask Dylan what he'd like to do?" It often seemed like I was the boy they wished their sons would choose for a friend. The other kids never said anything blatantly mean to me, but their actions told me silently that I wasn't part of the group. Sometimes I wished they'd just tell me to get lost.

Naturally, I had moved to this new town thinking for sure that I would meet another Jack. I never anticipated that having friends, even one friend, would be a constant battle that I didn't know why I was losing. I kept hoping against hope that maybe one day the neighborhood kids would magically say, "My mom is right! I'm gonna be best friends with Dylan!" and things would go back to the way they were when I hung out with Jack every day. The struggle to make friends in our new town proved to be more representative of what my life had in store for me.

One day in the summer of 1999, I was hysterically telling my mom that I didn't understand why the other boys never wanted to play in my backyard. She urged me to go along with whatever they were doing because I didn't have any friends. In a typical Asperger's moment, I insisted, "I have Jack!" My mom said very sternly, "Dylan—*you have to let go of Jack!*" Deep down I knew she was right. By that point Jack had moved to Pennsylvania, and I would never hear from him again. When I think back to that miserable summer, I can still hear my mom yelling, *"Let go of Jack!"*

This would not be the last time that my life saved the best for first. From third through fifth grades I was in a multi-age class, which meant you had the same teacher with the same group of students for three years. Ms. Woodward may have been the best teacher I ever had, and it was a nice group of kids, too.

People with Asperger's usually have a "special interest," a topic that we become obsessed with and gain encyclopedic knowledge about. I'd moved on from my childhood obsessions with vacuum cleaners, furnaces, *Star Wars,* and birds. By August 2000 my special interest had turned to pop music, but I was also very much interested in my female classmates.

As I began third grade in a new school, I immediately bonded with a girl named Brandi who had a cute face and blonde hair. She had a goofy, ADHD-style personality and she thought I was hilarious. Brandi was chubby in third grade and fourth grade. I don't know what she did in the summer before fifth grade, but she got thin and about a foot taller. I could tell she was really into me, but being ten years old I didn't realize that it was a crush. I'm sure it helped that I didn't get the memo. If I had, I would have started acting totally different and that would have been the end of that.

Brandi and I would sit together at lunch and joke around all the time. She had a cat named Millennium, (you know, like the Backstreet Boys album), and she also had a best friend named Hannah, who was pretty cute, too. I made friends with Tim and Evan, two of the boys in the class, and for a little while I was really tight with Kylie and Meredith, who were a grade ahead of me. I'm sure that being friends with those girls made me look really good, because they were older and more like the "popular girls."

During the three years in Ms. Woodward's class, I had a personal "ed-tech" whose job was being by my side in class, all day. Mrs. Gage was a much older woman in her sixties. I knew that the other kids in the class knew why Mrs. Gage was there and that one day, while I was out of the room, she and Ms. Woodward explained my issues to the whole class and asked them all to be patient with me. No matter what age you are, when everyone knows that you're the "special" kid and sees you getting disciplined for behavioral issues, it's never a bonus for attracting females.

I have to admit, they treated me pretty well at that school.

I didn't have to eat lunch in the cafeteria with everybody—I was allowed to pick a few people every day to hang back with me. The teachers and the kids I selected would eat lunch with me in the classroom. Every day I would either eat with Tim and Evan, Kylie and Meredith, or Brandi and Hannah. Giving me the choice to handpick the people I wanted to have lunch with made me feel less like a "special kid" and more like a boss. Even though Brandi and Hannah were always super-excited to eat lunch with me, they were usually the most boring. Tim and Evan were rowdy and fun, and Kylie and Meredith were so cool, and we would laugh the entire time. Again, not catching on that these girls were crushing on me all that time probably had everything to do with it.

By the time I was in fifth grade, Kylie and Meredith had graduated to middle school and, in turn, graduated from wanting to be my friends. I started hanging out with Brandi and Hannah more often because we thought the third and fourth graders were gross. I started thinking Brandi was a lot prettier, and I kind of liked her silly personality.

At the end of that year, I remember the three of us sitting together in art class talking about "who likes who." I would always bring up these conversations. Some things never change: unlike a lot of the boys, who took a long time to show any interest in girls (if they ever did), I had been bringing up "who likes who" since kindergarten. There we were in art class, sketching our watercolor impressions, and Brandi said, "Nobody likes me." Miraculously picking up on her hint, I said, "I wouldn't be so sure about that." If only my game was always as tight as it was in that moment! 😆

Before long we were using Hannah to go back and forth between us as the "he-said-she-said" messenger, because we were too scared to talk to each other. (Little did I know this must have been torture for her!) It was exactly what you would expect dating at eleven years old to be.

So as I finished elementary school I had my first girlfriend. I remember she gave me a handwritten letter spilling out all her feelings for me in very bubbly handwriting with a pink gel pen. I was on cloud nine, as happy as I'd ever been.

When I was at Brandi's house one day, we went to her room, and her parents made her keep the door cracked. There we were, the cutest tween couple in America, sitting on her bed watching *Lizzie McGuire*. Whenever her parents weren't looking, we would hold hands. Wow, what a thrill! I felt so badass. She said she had made out with her old boyfriend, and she probably wanted me to make out with her, but that level of hinting I couldn't quite pick up on yet. Besides, the handholding alone had me on the moon!

Just when I thought it couldn't get any better, one day when school ended, we all headed to get on our buses. Hannah pulled me aside and handed me a letter. It was even typed. I thought, "Wow, how fancy! She stepped it up a notch." I remember I really liked the font she used. (I got excited about fonts as a kid, another common autism interest.) Hannah told me it was Verdana and that she always used it. We had a little bonding moment. Her letter was more of a confession note, describing how over the last three years of knowing me she had fallen in love with me! "I am MADLY in love with you," she wrote three times. Now, this one took me by surprise! 😮

Hannah had hidden it a lot better than Brandi. I know you're probably laughing at the idea that any eleven-year-old kid could be in love, but you've got to remember that these girls had spent every day for three years knowing me. They didn't go through all this for any of the other boys in the class. Even though we were immature kids, developing feelings for someone over three years was more legit than a lot of relationships I've had since! Anyway, now Hannah wanted to be with me, too? I didn't know what to do! It was the best problem I ever had. In one moment I could not make up, I was talking to Hannah on AOL Instant Messenger (because it was 2003) and I asked if it would be cool with her if I had two girlfriends. Ha! I had so much to learn. 🧑

So, I pretty much spent summer 2003 dating Brandi for a week until she would find a reason to break up, and then I would date Hannah for a week, and Brandi would want me back, and so on. While the girls' feelings for me may have been legitimate, my knowledge of how to act like a boyfriend was not. My idea of how girls worked pretty much came from listening to pop songs on the radio and watching my favorite TV shows, like *Saved by the Bell*. If you were basing your knowledge of females on how they're presented in the media, you would think all girls wanted was a guy who would treat them nicely! *They're just so frustrated and tired of guys being jerks to them! Why can't they just find a guy who knows how to be a gentleman? That's all they want!*

Like my dad, it's my nature to be romantic, super-nice, and cute to a girl I like, so I figured I would be a great boyfriend, and we would last a long time. You can probably guess how long I kept these girls interested by being super-sweet to them. Like a cat you dangle a toy in front of, the second I dropped the toy and let them catch it, they got bored and lost interest. I had absolutely no idea why, and it completely devastated me. I was as upset when it ended as I'd been happy when it began.

Looking back now, it's no mystery at all why they broke up with me—I was acting lame! I was constantly telling them how wonderful they were and how happy I was to be with them. I stopped making myself any form of a challenge and started valuing them over anything else, even myself. I had a lot to learn, and it would be many years before I started understanding these things.

Still, nothing can take away the fact that over those three years, two girls simultaneously fell for me. To this day I have never had another situation like that. Now, before you start saying "Aww!" — what I mean is a situation in which a girl got to know me closely *over several years* and then fell for me. THAT never happened again. At the time, I had every reason to assume that the rest of life might be filled with times when a girl and I would get to know each other really well and then just gradually fall for each other, but it never happened again.

The environment of a multi-age elementary school classroom turned out to be more of a privilege than I ever realized. The real world is not quite as predictable, not nearly as structured, and there's no guarantee of an environment where you can build relationships over the course of several years. After the last bell rings, you find that people suddenly have a choice whether they stay in your world or not. Most people do not stick around as long as your peers in a multi-age classroom.

There's an old saying, "Save the best for last." Unfortunately, I have found that many times in my life, the best part came first.

The Short Bus and Middle School

I was basically kicked out of Sedgefield Middle School after the teachers and principal changed my IEP (Individualized Education Program) without even telling my parents. After discussing several options, my parents sent me to a school in the next town for kids with special needs. After a rough seventh grade year, they started transitioning me back into the public school. I went to Sedgefield Middle School in the morning and then, after a couple of classes, I was sent back to the special ed school. Transporting me meant that I had to be taken from school to school in a bus. But this was not just any regular bus, it was a *short bus*! A bright yellow short bus. I don't know what it's like where you live, but in Maine, riding on the short bus is only for the special ed kids. Actually, I'm pretty sure it's like that everywhere.

The school authorities arranged for me to be picked up right outside the front of the school, all by myself, in the middle of the day. I was not happy about the prospect of my peers seeing me board a short bus in broad daylight; this was a non-starter. I asked, "Can the bus please pick me up just 50 feet down the road, on the side of the school instead of in front of the grand entrance?" Thankfully after much unnecessary negotiation, we won that battle and it was arranged for me to leave through the rear entrance behind the gym. There was no way I was going to get on that short bus with the possibility of some cute seventh-grade girl looking out the window.

People always talk about how difficult middle school is, but I think I can tell you the reason middle school in particular sucks so much. It's the age where kids are developed enough to be cliquey, socially selective, and judgmental, but they aren't old enough to have a sense of politeness and courtesy for others. If the totem pole for social value was the internet, middle school would be the '90s. Middle school is the America Online, it's the dial-up of social hierarchy. As we mature, even in high school, we start to have some manners, and we become a little more considerate. As adults, we develop very sophisticated ways of rejecting people. If we're at a party and someone is making conversation with us but we don't want to talk to them, we might make just enough conversation to be polite, or we might pretend to save their phone number. But a middle school kid will just blankly stare at you without speaking, and then walk away. It's the '90s internet! Remember when you used to type one wrong letter and it would take you to some adult spam site? There's no real sense of social hierarchy before puberty, so elementary school is like pre-internet. But middle school is pure animalistic social rank. It's about who's cool, who's weird, and that's all that matters. That's what makes middle school so tough.

Counselors and Teachers

Because I was such a complex and difficult child with so many behavioral issues, teachers and educational staff always played a much larger role in my life than in most kids'. There's nothing better than a good teacher and nothing worse than a bad one. In second grade my teacher was a woman named Mrs. Weebler, who was so bad it was comical. She was in her sixties, and the year I was in her class was actually her last year before retiring, and it showed. She would scream at us, throw books across the room, and kick chairs. 😄 It was like a bad reality show; my mom offered to have me switched to another teacher midway through the year, but Mrs. Weebler's antics provided me so much entertainment value that I wanted to stay. I went from one extreme to the other the next year when I had the aforementioned Ms. Woodward and my ed-tech Mrs. Gage, who were both fantastic. I think the two qualities that make for a good teacher are sincerity and good communication skills. I know it sounds crazy, but there are many teachers who make it absolutely clear they don't enjoy working with kids. Or if they do, you can't tell. And you should be able to tell, it shouldn't even be a question. The obvious question is: why are they teachers? I have no idea. I can tell you though, the fact that teachers are virtually unable to be fired is a *huge* problem that's affecting *your* children, and it needs to be fixed in this country.

With my personality of seeking controversy and pushing the limits—there are some people I really rub the wrong way. At the special school I was sent to for behavioral issues in seventh grade, my teacher, Eden (they went by first names), was one of those people who really seemed to dislike my personality. It happens: not everyone is going to like you, right? But when you're being ruled over by someone who doesn't like you, needless to say, it's a bad situation. Luckily Sheryl, one of the ed-techs in my room, had a personality that was Eden's opposite. She was easy-going, had a sense of humor, and liked me; I always wondered what she really thought of Eden's totalitarian style of discipline. In my second year there, they brought in another ed-tech appropriately named Dick, and that was when things really got scary. Dick had absolutely no business working with any kids, let alone special needs kids. He played in a band, and I tried to befriend him by making small talk with him about music during breaks, but you couldn't win with him. He was just a mean guy. If I so much as laughed at something he didn't like during class, he'd send me into the hall, where Eden would leave me for the duration of the school day. I knew this instinctively at the time, and looking back it's even clearer to me now: these were people who disliked me on a very gut level, abusing their power over me.

In high school, I lucked out being in the resource room with Mr. Topsham, a down-to-earth, very sincere guy who liked me. However, after having me in his class for a while, his patience with me began wearing thin as well.

I remember having a conversation with my mom at the time and she told me something that remains true: I seem to have a pattern of wearing people down to the point where they throw up their hands and want nothing to do with me. She pointed out that the same thing had happened with Mrs. Gage in elementary school and with Eden in middle school (albeit she just went from disliking me to despising me). She said I should do my best to figure out what it is about me that has that effect on people. I believe it has to do with me being so intense, but then the question is: why do some people like that for a while and only over time grow tired of it? 🤔

Throughout my entire public school career, I was put in the dreaded "social skills groups" run by the school guidance counselor or social worker. These groups purported to teach you social skills with which to better interact with your peers, but what they delivered was an absolute joke—every single one of them. I may not have been adept at social skills as a kid, but you don't have to be good at something to know it when you see it. And I knew that going up to another eighth grade student and offering a handshake while saying, "Hi, my name is Dylan," wasn't going to get me far, even if I maintained eye contact while I did it! Among the issues with these groups were that the special needs kids of all functional levels were thrown in together, forcing them to cater to the lowest-functioning student in the group, while the rest of us just sat there thinking, "At least we got to skip class . . ."

Even if it had been advice tailored to higher-functioning individuals, these classes were run by fifty-five-year-olds who hadn't been in high school since Disco Demolition Night. I think as adults, we have a hard time accepting that we might not be able to give social skills advice to young people. Nobody likes feeling old. I don't think it's personal—I think once we reach a certain age we simply cannot remember what it was really like out there in the trenches, as much as we might believe otherwise. *It seems like just yesterday I was in school myself, and I can remember what it was like, enough to give advice. I'd have to be stupid not to be able to help out someone struggling with social skills; after all, I do just fine getting along with people.* I think we forget that mindset of being fifteen and interacting with other fifteen-year-olds. There is a certain way teenagers interact that's different from how adults interact. It is faster-paced, there are higher expectations, and less forgiveness.

The question is, do schools really want to help students struggling to fit in? Or is it more important to them to stick to protocol? If schools really want to help, I think they should enlist students with high social value to work undercover and give special needs kids a leg up. These students could either offer advice behind closed doors, or they could do things like openly showing friendliness to a special needs student around school or even including them at their table in the cafeteria. Oftentimes all it takes is one person, and then everyone else will follow. But instead of taking that suggestion seriously, most schools will surely ignore it as they continue putting forth baby boomers to give advice to teenagers.

Developing the skills to fit in when you don't is a truly complex and difficult task, and it's more of an art than a science. I truly believe advice MUST come from a peer to be effective. I'm sorry, getting old sucks!

The Mar

One of my earliest memories was a warm afternoon in 1997. I got off the school bus, and my mom was there waiting for me.

"Do you want to go get a cat?" she asked.

We had a dog then that I was very fond of, so I was totally happy to get another pet. As we arrived at the now-defunct Marlee Animal Shelter, I first experienced the joy of being surrounded by the most beautiful animals in the world. Anyone who has ever visited an animal shelter knows the stark contrast between the dog room and the cat room. For someone on the autism spectrum, unless you really, really love dogs, the dog room is hell on your senses. It's a dark, poorly-sanitized, foul-smelling warehouse full of dogs barking at the top of their lungs—lunging out at you, only to crash up against the chain fences of their cages, and then bark louder. If you like animals at all, you will feel very bad for the dogs, but you will also feel like your ears are bleeding.

As we walked through the dog area and then into the cat room, it was like night and day. In the cat room was pin-dropping silence. It was brightly lit and remarkably clean. I was comfortable there. I had seen cats before, but now we were picking out a cat to adopt, so I was really paying attention and I was absolutely struck by their beauty. 🐱 I had been to church many times as a child, but as I witnessed these elegant, achingly gorgeous, infinitely perfect creatures, I knew there must be a God. ⛪

Some of the cats were poking their paws out to greet us, some of them were sleeping, some of them were meowing to say hello. I wanted to take all of them home! My mom, however, reminded me we were there to get only one. I carefully surveyed my options. I opened one cage with a large gray cat. She hissed at us like we were enemy cats in her territory. We opened another cage. Inside it was a beautiful orange tabby that looked like Garfield. As I reached my hand in, he coughed and sneezed like he was dying. The poor baby was very sick!

We had looked at almost every cat when my mom said to me, "Well, Dylan, what about this one?" It was a small, quiet, female cat that we had overlooked while all the other cats worked to get our attention. She was a shorthaired tabby. She was very cute, and as I picked her up out of her cage, it was clear she was also very sweet. As soon I held her, I was in awe of her remarkably soft coat. She settled in my arms like a newborn baby (except much cuter) and I began to pet her. She started purring, and it was a done deal: this was the one who would be joining our family!

As we walked out of the shelter with my new cat in her carrier, we looked back at the sign, "Marlee Animal Shelter." We had found the perfect name for our new friend—Marlee!

The cat was beautiful inside and out, and I affectionately nicknamed her "The Mar." The Mar was an exceptional cat. She was very good with my then three-year-old sister, Mariah, and six-year-old me, who wanted to pet her and play with her 'round the clock. The Mar didn't seem to mind as we paraded her through the house, dressed her up in silly costumes, and took pictures of her. I particularly took to The Mar and was so overcome with her beauty that she made me forget that we had dogs.

Whenever I went to someone's house, if they had a cat, I would get very excited, assuming their cat must be just like mine. I found that other cats would hiss if you tried to pick them up, swat you if you tried to pet them, or simply run away frantically if you approached them. I realized The Mar was special. I cherished her and showered her with love. I began feeding her in my room. I got a special bed just for her, as well as a scratchpad and catnip toys—my room was totally tricked-out for The Mar. I slept with her every night next to me. And that was how I realized the truth of the expression: "Cats are man's best friend."

Special Interests

Probably the biggest hallmark of autism, is what they call the "special interests"—when an autistic individual becomes captivated with a subject and it's all they want to talk about. There are great things about learning so much about a single topic, but there are challenges that you may not realize. You might see a child having such an incredible grasp on one topic as cute, and say, "What a talented young man! So enthusiastic about learning! He has a bright future ahead of him!"

That's not necessarily the case though. The way the world works is that if your interest doesn't translate into a lucrative career, or at least a job where you can put it to use, it's useless. And not only does it serve no purpose, it can turn your childhood into an especially lonely experience. It was often difficult for me to find peers to talk to about whatever I was obsessed with and share my knowledge with them.

As a child it often felt like my only friend was my encyclopedia of Billboard Hot 100 Hits.

My unique special interests have always been a struggle. If you learn one thing from me, let it be this: if you know a kid who's going through this—a kid dealing with an obsession—realize that it might be very frustrating for them and that they probably want to talk to somebody about it. The next time you meet someone with autism who has a special interest, Wikipedia a few facts and have a conversation with them. I promise you'll make their day.

Some of my interests were harder for people to relate to than others. I went through a period in elementary school when I was obsessed with cars. It was easy to talk to people about cars, even other kids—I could just ask them what their parents drove! (I remember Brandi's parents both had Saturns, R.I.P.) And I could tell people more about their car than they knew! So that was pretty fun.

My biggest and longest-lasting special interest has been music. Now, you may think, "Who doesn't want to talk about music? Everybody loves music." If I were in front of a large group of people and asked, "How many of you would like to have a conversation with me after the show about music?"—a lot of hands might go up. But if I asked, "How many of you would like to have a conversation about Katy Perry's last album, and whether they released the right singles for radio airplay, and how the production fits in with trends we're seeing in the current music climate"—probably not as many hands would go up. In fact, I'd be lucky if one hand went up.

My interest in music has always been about obsessing over the creative and commercial aspects of pop music—not exactly things most people enjoy discussing or analyzing. People love music, but sadly most people don't respect pop music. They view it kind of like candy, a guilty pleasure they might enjoy now and then, but certainly not something they would ever think of delving into deep conversations about.

Pop music has always been my first love. I love pop music more than cats, more than food, even more than hot girls. As I look back through my life, what was playing on the radio was always more important to me than anything going on in my own life. Growing up in the late '90s, hearing the Spice Girls and the Backstreet Boys coming through the speakers of my mom's Grand Caravan had me in love for life. I'm going to stop myself right now because I could go on about the history of pop music for the rest of this book. Don't worry though, you will be seeing plenty of references. And if you are the one person in the world who is interested in learning about pop music, there's a bonus chapter available at BadChoicesMakeGoodStories.com! 🙂 Send me an email too, I would like to know who you are! RealDielawn@gmail.com

The Adventures of High School: Dielawn Is Born

2006–Freshman Year of High School

My freshman year of high school was a bad time of my life. Looking back, there was really nothing that could have made it better. At age fourteen, I could be very abrasive, and I had a long way to go in terms of social skills, but neurotypical fourteen-year-olds were sometimes as difficult to deal with as I was. I was able to have perfectly good conversations with adults. My history teacher and I got along great! So, it wasn't *all* on my end.

As I have said, conversations in high school are very fast-paced, and kids' talking style is very different from the style of adult conversations. To use a sports analogy, adult conversations are like baseball: very orderly, very organized. Trying to join a group of adults in conversation would be like trying to join a base-ball game at your local park. (I don't know this, but I'm guessing you would just walk up and ask to join—not that hard.)

A conversation with teenagers is like basketball. Wherever the ball goes, it goes. It's not orderly—it's chaotic. And trying to follow every move the players make is more challenging than a baseball game. So trying to join a conversation as a kid is like trying to jump into the middle of a basketball game and start playing.

And if you're reading this, thinking, "That sounds easy," or "That would be fun," then you definitely don't have Asperger's. Most people like the basketball style of conversation as kids, and then somewhere in their late-teens/early twenties gradually evolve to the baseball style. I won't speak for all people on the autism spectrum, but I came out of the womb not being able to follow a basketball game, so my childhood was bound to be rough.

Ironically, it took my getting older before I learned how to be a kid.

As a high school freshman, I had very little in common with my peers and no real way to relate to them. Most people on the spectrum are born as little adults, and I was no exception. What was I going to talk to a kid about? My life at that point was listening to talk radio shows and '80s' pop music. I did have enough sense *not* to approach the popular jocks in my school with a conversation comparing Paula Abdul's first and second albums. (*Forever Your Girl* vs. *Spellbound* anyone?) Thank God, by the time I was a senior, I had become interested in normal teenage things.

For my eighth grade graduation dance, I had managed to land a date with a cute girl named Kelly. Kelly, her friend Kaylee, and I had then become friends for a short period of time and hung out for my birthday over the summer. Once high school started even the girls were drifting apart from each other as Kelly started hanging out with all the theater kids. I failed to recognize that we didn't have much of a connection: whatever friendship we had last year was last year. They were nice girls who weren't going to be rude—most people will never come out and say they don't want to be friends with you. They'll say whatever you want to hear and then do the opposite. It took me a while to accept that people truly speak with their actions.

On the other hand, I had reconnected with my old buddy from elementary school, Tim. After my return to middle school, Tim and I had started talking one day as we were making fun of a beta-male motivational speaker the school had us listen to. Over the summer we had started hanging out regularly again, and we always had a blast. We had a similar sense of humor, and we had fun together watching shows like *Crank Yankers* and *Jackass*. I was really upset when freshman year started and I quickly began hearing from him less and less. He was really trying to fit into the jock crowd. I didn't see the big picture then, which is that Tim was just trying to look out for himself. None of the kids he played football with saw me as cool, and it would have cost him social status to be seen hanging out with me.

By Christmas break of that year, I was fresh out of friends. There had been a brief window of time over the summer when I had a social life, and now it seemed like it had all been a tease. My life reverted to what it had been before, a lonely existence of isolation from my peers. I went to a school with a thousand kids, and I saw everyone else, even the weird kids, hanging out with their own cliques. I may as well have not existed. It didn't help that it was the dead of winter, either. December and January are cold and bleak in Maine. It can be pitch dark by 4:30 p.m. That can be depressing no matter who you are.

For many people going through hardship, music can be an escape. During those dark times, it was Madonna who shined a "Ray of Light" (get it?) into my world. A couple of years back, Sheryl, the cool ed-tech at that school I was sent to for seventh grade, had burned me a CD of Madonna's 2005 album, *Confessions On a Dance Floor*.

During my freshman year, I finally put it on one day and pressed "play." My jaw stayed dropped for an hour straight. The album was amazing from start to finish. I love any music with a sassy female singing over a dance beat—that is my sh*t! I have always loved Madonna, and *Confessions* is her best work. It's still one of those albums I would take with me if I was stranded on a desert island (I would probably also try to smuggle *Headstrong* by Ashley Tisdale.) Living with autism, it often feels like my special interests are my only friend. And during the friend-desert that was my freshman year of high school, this album was just what I needed to keep me company.

A Disney Cruise Gives Me a Glimpse of What's Possible

In April 2007, my family took a Disney cruise. If you have never been on a cruise, they always have a lounge where just teenagers can hang out. There were about thirty kids, with lots of cute females and guys that looked straight out of the popular crowd at my high school. And then there was my sister and me. I was fifteen, and Mariah was thirteen.

I figured it wouldn't be much different from high school, and I would probably have only my sister to hang out with, but I was always up for a challenge.

There were games and activities (supervised by adults, obviously). One night we were playing trivia with the guys against the girls. As luck would have it, a question came up about '80s' music: "Name the artist of the song from *Dirty Dancing*—'(I've Had) The Time of My Life.'"

We were supposed to talk it over among our team, but f*ck *that!* I sprang into action and yelled, "Bill Medley and Jennifer Warnes!" The guy holding the trivia card was stunned and yelled, "Oh my God, nobody's ever gotten that right in the five years I've worked here!"

I knew he wasn't lying: most people who lived through the '80s might not remember Bill Medley and Jennifer Warnes. I have a photographic memory, especially for pop music, so I could literally see a picture in my head of this song printed on the charts of my *Billboard Hot 100* books. All the many hours I spent obsessing over the top songs of 1987 paid off. The trivia guy was so impressed, he ran out of the room and grabbed me a Disney Teen Club T-shirt as a prize. That was the first moment the other kids started to notice me.

Later we were doing a dance contest where everybody had to come up with a silly dance move. I am *not* a dancer. My lack of rhythm certainly proves the stereotype that white people can't dance. When it was my turn, I froze. It's not like me to choke in front of people, so I had to pull out something. I broke out into a crazy mess of waving my hands in and out like I was swimming, and making a face by sucking in my cheeks and pressing my lips together like a fish. One thing I learned from after-school theater classes is that you have to *commit* to the moment. I went all in with this dance, and every kid in the place burst out laughing. Actually, I'm not sure if it was *every* kid, but it was the kids that mattered. In a group setting, there are certain people who are the tastemakers for the group. When you win them over, everyone else follows suit.

In that one moment, my status skyrocketed, from just some guy there in the background to becoming the center of attention. The other kids all started calling me "Fish," which was not my ideal nickname, but I wasn't complaining. 😂

I was literally a superstar for the next three or four days on that cruise. Whenever I appeared, everybody started yelling out, "Fish!" Once I'm established as "the funny guy," people see that I'm a natural entertainer who doesn't know how *not* to be funny. The more you pay attention to me, the more you're going to laugh. All it takes is me getting in the door. On that Disney cruise, I'd busted that door open. Getting this much attention might overwhelm a lot of people, but I'm overwhelmed when I'm *not* the center of attention. Everybody was following me around wanting to talk to me. They weren't just including me in conversation—I *was* the conversation.

It all culminated on the final night. We had karaoke in the ship's nightclub. Everyone was begging me to do a song. I went up and sang Sisqo's "Thong Song." I don't remember much about it, but I recall that I was really goofy, and everybody was eating it up.

When I got off the stage, I ended up sitting on a couch between a bunch of girls and the popular guys. It was so far from my life back home. It made it even better to have my sister there witnessing it all, perfectly happy to fall into the background and let me have my moment. Also, Mariah would be able to testify on my behalf if anyone doubted that it really happened.

The whole week was more dreamlike than most dreams I've ever had. I remember wishing I could have stayed on that cruise ship forever. I knew that on Monday I wouldn't be able to go up to the popular jocks at school and say, "No, no, no . . . you guys don't understand . . . I was *the* most popular kid on this cruise ship!" 😶

Why was I experiencing a week as a rock star, only to leave and go back to a high school where nobody knew I existed? Was I inside a *Twilight Zone* episode? I kept waiting for Rod Serling to come out and say, "Dylan Seth Volk, an awkward teenager whose only friend was his favorite Madonna CD, until he set sail on a

Disney cruise . . . to the Twilight Zone."

As I was telling my mom about everything that happened, (with my sister backing me up so she believed it) she gave me a perspective that made it better. I'll never forget her saying, "That just shows what is possible!" I thought the same thing, but I was very reassured to hear her say it. That was one of those rare moments that just shut me up.

Summer 2007: Back to Reality

The summer of 2007 sucked, period. If I thought making friends in my freshman year was hard, the summer that followed freshman year was *b-r-u-t-a-l*. Running on my school's cross-country team was almost my only opportunity to interact with anybody that summer. When I stopped to tie my shoe, the two guys I was running with took the opportunity to take off on me and pretend not to hear me when I yelled, "Wait up!" That felt really great. Kirk was the only kid slower and fatter than me, and yet even he blew me off when given the chance.

Another kid, Bryan, lived in my neighborhood. He was a preppy dude who played in a rock band and was always down to hang out with me. He seemed kind of cool, but we had absolutely nothing in common and usually nothing to talk about. Yet, he was strangely willing to come over and even go places with my parents and me. It hit me years later that he was possibly an in-the-closet gay guy. I think he was hoping something would happen with us. I don't know where he got that idea, I guess it could have been my insisting we watch new episodes of *Kathy Griffin: My Life On The D List*. Who knows?

My focus was beginning to shift from chasing after friendship to chasing after girls. I had always had a "someday . . . " attitude, when it came to girls. I saw other guys with girlfriends, holding hands, making out in the hallways, and I just figured someday that would be me.

The night of my sixteenth birthday, I had an epiphany. I was sitting in bed, reflecting on my life, as I do so well, counting down the minutes. As I figuratively took a good look in the mirror, I saw a dorky kid with braces who still hadn't had his first kiss, and all of a sudden it hit me that in just two short years, the teenage girls that drove me so crazy would be off limits. *For the record and to be very clear*, no, I am not attracted to females unless they are at least twenty now, but when I was sixteen, you'd better believe I was. In my sixteen-year-old brain, spending the rest of my life not knowing what a sixteen-year-old girl felt like was such a terrifying thought, it jolted me up off my pillow like in the movies when someone wakes up from a dream!

I asked myself, "What was I expecting?" Was I thinking I would just wake up one day with the head of the cheering team on my lap? It wasn't just that I wanted to get some action. I understood that when a girl hooks up with you, she's saying you're good enough. You made the cut. I wanted a girl to say that with her *actions*. I did *not* want to wait until I was older to be appreciated. I was in a race against time—the time to f*ck around was vanishing.

My entire focus in life became getting my first kiss while I was still sixteen. At that time, I felt like sixteen was the last acceptable age to have your first anything. I was dead set on making it happen. Did I have a clue how to talk to girls? Nope! But there I was, throwing absolutely anything at the wall. This was one of the most cringe-worthy periods of my life (that's saying something), full of many colorful, misguided attempts to holler at females. 👤

For your sake, I will only cover some of the highlights. Looking back, the first move I made was actually pretty smart. I knew that I wasn't ready to step to females that I actually went to school with. I decided I would do some good, old focus group testing.

Back before they really started cracking down on perverts, there was a super-sketchy website called TeenSpot, "A place where teens can connect!" It should have been promoted as "A place where teens can get ratchet!" because that's what it was. I grabbed my dad's digital camera (remember those?), took some mirror selfies, and got to work.

Obviously, TeenSpot was never on the level of Facebook

or even MySpace, so the girls you met on there were just from random places, looking for something they weren't getting where they lived. This was a zero-risk way for me to test out what it's like flirting with girls. It seems lame now, but having no experience in real life at that point, it was very exciting to get called "cute" online by a girl from Missouri. Now, I know you're thinking, "What if she was a seventy-year-old man?!" I hate to break it you, folks: those stories make for good TV, but the reality is that even a sixteen-year-old with Asperger's can easily spot a fake profile online.

After a few months of "cybermackin" on lonely girls from the flyover states, I decided to try out my new skills in the big leagues. There was a girl named Ashlyn English in my town who was always friendly to me, so I thought I had a shot with her. I made a video where I rapped her name by each letter, like "A cuz she's A-list swag, S all that sass and she ain't even black," etc. At the end of the video I asked her out on a date to the movies that weekend. I put it on a new video website called YouTube and sent it to her. I must have misread our "friendship" because she didn't even respond.

I felt very embarrassed and took it down a week later, but not before everyone in town had seen it and laughed at it, of course. This multiplied by hundreds whatever embarrassment I had felt when she didn't comment. But looking back, I'm not that ashamed. With girls, I feel like it's infinitely better to be too bold than not bold enough. I'd like to know if Ashlyn dated any other guys with the balls to pull a romantic stunt like that to win her attention.

From that point on, I just stayed away from girls in my town. I knew nothing good would happen if everyone I went to school with knew about my trials and many errors cutting my teeth with females. Unfortunately, I didn't have much luck with girls in other towns, either. I was endlessly messaging girls on MySpace and AIM but it was just one dead end after another. The few times I did manage to get a girl to agree to meet up, I ended up wishing I stayed home.

One of the times I thought I'd have some success was with

a girl from Biddeford, about a half-hour away. I was supposed to meet her at the movies. She never showed up. I didn't have a driver's license yet, so the icing on the cake was calling my mom to come back and get me.

Another time, I went to meet this other chick at a high school football game in another town. I had to spend two hours following her group of friends around. None of them knew me, and they had no interest in getting to know me. It didn't take me much time dealing with females to realize that "it ain't like the movies." 😟

I hadn't had any luck socially yet, but not everything in my life was a disaster. The now-defunct Comedy Connection in Portland, Maine, had a workshop. For ten weeks you met once a week, and they helped you develop a comedy act. Unlike my social life where everything went wrong, this was the one place where everything went right. It was a group of mostly older people, and I was the quirky young kid who impressed everybody.

The reason I don't mind bragging like that is because making people laugh has always been the only thing I'm really good at. The second week of the workshop, a journalist from *Salt*, a local magazine, was observing us for an article she was writing about comedy. After Pamela saw me perform my material, she pulled me aside and asked me some questions. Apparently she knew all about Asperger's and had diagnosed me on sight. After our talk, she decided to refocus the article on me!

It was an interesting time for someone to be covering my life. I was sixteen and had my first job. I had no idea how to separate the guy I was on stage from the guy I was supposed to be at work. One day, a black guy who looked like Barack Obama walked into the pizza shop. I yelled, "Hey, we got Barack Obama in the house! Get that man a pizza . . . Hawaiian-style!" The black guy was visibly flattered and started laughing, but all my *white* coworkers seemed very offended. (I have lived all around the country, and have found that people in Maine get offended more easily than any place else. They really need to lighten up.)

It was also at that job where one of the waitresses got a botched boob job. My jokes about her distorted breasts were the final straw that would soon lead to my getting fired. However, before they fired me, the owner was nice enough to let Pamela come in and shadow me. She also interviewed some of my coworkers. They had some interesting things to say. None of them could figure me out.

Finally, the night of the live comedy performance arrived. That day at school, I had flyers about the event and intended to hand them out to a few teachers who liked me. I was at lunch, as usual sitting at whichever table looked like it had the smallest number of haters, when Nick, this tall blond dude, came by and started talking about a party he was having. What came into my mind immediately: party equals girls. I did what anybody desperate for friends and females would do—I invited myself!

To my surprise, he didn't shoot me down. He asked me what I had in my hand, and I told him I was in a comedy show that night in Portland. I suggested that he should come, and we could go to the party from there. I was boldly putting myself out there because I was starring in a comedy show and, while that was all fun and great, it was November 2007 and I *still* hadn't kissed a girl. That took priority over everything. I never needed a reminder that I hadn't reached this milestone. Every girl I saw in the halls of my high school made me think, "Why aren't we making out?" I had to make this happen.

Now, out of nowhere, this popular guy was going let me come to a party—a real high school house party like I had heard about and seen on TV! It almost seemed too good to be true. Sure enough, the night of the final performance, Nick showed up *and* brought his homeboy. Wow, I guess I really sold it to him! Nick was the kind of kid I could take one look at and tell he was popular. He partied hard and with everybody. Girls wanted to be with him, guys wanted to be him, he was the man. My parents and his parents had actually known each other since Nick and I were really little. At that time, he was a wild and hyper kid that I could never keep up with.

I was about to get on stage for the comedy set that I had

developed in a ten-week comedy workshop! After all that practice, I *killed.* I did jokes about school, girls and teachers, but the one joke that really knocked it out of the park was a story I told about being at a family gathering, and meeting my third cousin, who was super-hot. I then said, "I was getting on Wikipedia to see if a third cousin qualified as incest . . . 'cause after all, we were up in northern Maine."

After the show Nick and his friend took me for a ride in his mom's Lexus. From the first night of hanging out with this guy, I could tell this was a good connection to have. Nick knew a lot of people and, even better, a lot of girls. As it turned out, Nick was a pro at hooking up with girls. Not only that, but he was down to help me out with my problem!

Fast-forward a few weeks later. Nick hit me up on AIM saying he had a girl he wanted me to meet. Her name was Amy (which was and still is weird, because that's my mom's name). Without giving the details, on a cold December night in 2007 in the back of a 2001 Mazda Protege, I didn't just get my first kiss, I got my first everything. And wait for the twist . . . she was twenty-one years old!!! *A twenty-one-year-old was my first time.* Thank you, Nick! Now, this was a friend. He could have never talked to me again and I would still be grateful forever that he hooked it up for me.

In one night I literally went from not having even touched a girl outside of a school dance to having covered more bases than half the guys in my class! 😄 I felt great about myself. My confidence shot through the roof, and it's a good thing it happened when it did.

"Just Be Yourself"

One piece of advice that I have received throughout my life is, "Just be yourself." When neurotypical people say that, I always think, "Well, that's easy for you to say." But it's totally useless advice for someone with autism! When people say that, I feel like they're suggesting I should be able to just kick back and expect everything in life to simply fall into place.

What I have come to realize is that this is advice from neuro-typical people, for neurotypical people. When you guys say this to each other, you instinctively understand the nuance in this phrase. You know that "just be yourself" doesn't mean that you can be the same person on a Friday night at the club with friends, as you are on a Wednesday afternoon eating lunch with your coworkers. To those of us with a black and white brain, "Just be yourself" means no filter needed. There's an episode of *Friends* in which Chandler is going on a date, and Phoebe tells him "Just remember, be your-self—Oh! But not too much."

One of my first recollections putting this advice to use was at the pizza shop, when I made the Obama-Hawaiian pizza joke. In hindsight, although it was funny, I get that it wasn't workplace-appropriate. But was that me being myself? You bet. Not everyone can just be themselves and expect social success. I have realized as I've gotten older that everyone modifies their behavior to fit the circumstances they're in. Neurotypicals just do it better than those of us on the spectrum.

Here is my advice to anyone with autism (or if you know someone with autism): you can be yourself in keeping with your inner self, meaning your morals and your values. Be yourself by remaining true to your character. But as far as everything on the outside: the way you talk, the things you say, the way you dress—you don't have to "just be yourself." It's okay to play around and switch things up to see what works—everybody does—it's just that some people are much better actors than others. Most people don't even realize when they're doing it, it just comes naturally to them. So my Obama reference was "Nail Number One" in my proverbial coffin, with "Nail Number Two" to follow soon, when I joked about the waitress who had had the "enhancement." Word soon got around that there were many more inappropriate comments coming from the same person. Things were not looking good for me.

When the pizza place finally decided to fire me, they actually called my mom and asked her to fire me for them. When I learned about this later, I found it extremely cowardly, but at the time, I didn't know what was happening.

My mom told the manager, "No. You can fire him. I'll bring him over there, and I'll walk him in, and then you can tell him what's going on. You hired him. You can fire him. You run a business and manage people. You're an adult. I think you can handle firing a sixteen-year-old boy."

I'm glad my mom did that. She drove me over there, and I kind of knew that something was up. I could tell that I was in trouble. I knew she was pissed, but I had no idea they were going to fire me. I had no sense of self-awareness and really needed a wake-up call. That was my first cold, hard lesson, because I really liked that job! I liked the people I worked with, and I liked the work I was doing—the best of both worlds—but I only had it for two months before I blew it. I honestly had no idea how inappropriate I was being. This was my first dose of workplace reality. I started thinking, "Wow, maybe this job thing is not going to be as easy as I thought."

"Why Can't I Dress Like That?"

DISCLAIMER: Please place this in the context of what was purely a comedy routine at the time, aimed at making high school kids laugh. I know that my making fun of disabled people was unkind and offensive to many people. I apologize in advance to anyone who may be offended.

Freshman year was not all bad. There was one group I was able to connect with. As a kid growing up, I never felt I had a style that fit me. I wore whatever my mom picked out for me. In other words, I had zero swag. Even in my suburban Maine town, there were plenty of kids who dressed in an urban style, spoke with urban slang, listened to rap music, and so on. I never saw myself fitting in with those types of crowds. In my freshman year, I had taken Speech and Debate as an elective class. There was a dude in the class who was a senior named Josh, who was cool as hell. Despite having the whitest of names, Josh was the definition of what some might disparagingly refer to as a "wigger"—like

I said, he was cool as hell.

Every morning before school, as everyone was congregating around their lockers and socializing, the special ed teachers would swing open the back doors of the hallway and bring through all the disabled kids in their wheelchairs. Everyone would clear off to the sides and allow the wheelchairs to pass through, in the fashion of a parade. One day after school, I went up to Josh and his friends at their lockers to see if I could make them laugh. It was my only way to have a chance at being friends with a guy like Josh. He was standing there with a bunch of seniors, so I figured I would go up to them and test out a little bit of a *highly* politically incorrect comedy routine that I had developed from observing this parade of special ed kids every morning. I had nothing to lose, right? It was a bunch of senior guys. It's not like they were likely to hang out with a geeky freshman anyway.

I went up and started talking: "Every morning, isn't it like a 'parade of the 'tards?' They got the wheelchairs comin' through like a major event. Everybody gets off to the side and lets the 'tards get their shine on for a minute." I followed that up by mimicking the special ed kids, with all the physical gestures and noises they make. I suggested maybe adding some trumpets to signify that "the 'tards are coming through!" and then maybe some theme music for the 'tard parade!

This would have fallen flat on all the popular, sports-obsessed preppy kids in my class, but it was considered a riot by these guys. They started laughing hysterically and even got out a flip phone (it was 2006, after all) and told me to say it again, so they could get it on video.

Josh actually ended up kind of being friends with me. He even invited me to skip school one time to drive around with him and his friends. Well, okay, it was technically just lunch period, but it still felt pretty badass for me at the time. Here I was, some dorky freshman, and I was skipping lunch period with some awesome seniors! I look back on this time as the first seed that was planted in my head, that maybe kids like Josh or Nick, whom I would have written off as the "burnout" crowd before, just might be people who could appreciate me. To use a movie reference, it was like *The Breakfast Club*, and I always thought I had to win over Emilio Estevez's character; I never even considered trying to befriend Judd Nelson's character. From there, I started thinking about the way I presented myself and the way I dressed. Instead of trying to look like the guys who wore polos and khakis, I started looking at guys who wore fitted hats and baggy clothes, like, "Wait, why can't I dress like that?"

As time went by I started realizing that I actually had more I could identify with among these kids than with the popular crowd. The popular kids had gone through life having friends, getting good grades, and excelling in sports. Why did I think I could relate to them? Meanwhile a lot of kids like Nick or Josh, not unlike John Bender in *The Breakfast Club*, hadn't had the best upbringings. And while that wasn't the same struggle I knew, struggle comes in many forms. At a certain point I realized as far as being accepted, I was better off with people who had been through some kind of struggle of their own.

(Almost) Kicked Out of Boarding School

When it came to school, I was absolutely drowning. The only reason I did okay freshman year was that I was sheltered all year in a resource room, where I had little to no homework. In my sophomore year, they decided I needed to take on more mainstream classes, with disastrous results. I couldn't keep up with the note-taking, the homework and the fast pace. I don't know how you neurotypical people do it, but hats off to you. My parents decided that the school "wouldn't admit that they were in over their head" with me, so they took me out of public high school. After one visit to a boarding school three hours away in northern New Hampshire, they decided to send me there. What we will call Mount Snow Academy was a very small school with about thirty kids. Every single student except me was a neurotypical kid, and most seemed to be there for drug rehabilitation.

At Mount Snow Academy, I developed a gift for pissing people off. The school director gave me an analogy about how most people enter conversations. He said most people join conversations like they're entering a crowded room, they peek in, and then slowly and quietly wander in. He said when I entered conversations I was like a firefighter busting down the door. If only I could have understood that analogy at the time.

I spent a month at the school basically getting into arguments with every student. Most of the arguments stemmed from of my own frustrations because I had no idea how to fit in. What I really wanted was to know how to effortlessly be included in social interactions, like every other student there. But I didn't have that skill, so instead I would start sh*t with people just for the human interaction.

Grant was the biggest guy there. He was also the most popular and well-respected. He was dating a really cute chick, probably the hottest girl (out of all nine of them) at Mount Snow. One day I saw them in the dark, making out like their plane was going down. In high school, seeing this type of thing hurt me to my core, because that was what I wanted to have with someone. I hated to see other people have it. The (not) very smart way I handled Grant and his girlfriend was to interrupt them and tell them they had to cut out the PDA (public displays of affection). Looking back, Grant was the type of alpha male that I could have easily been cool with, but instead I ended up almost getting into a fistfight. The school staff had to come running to intervene. Grant, still furious, ran off and punched a glass window.

I had no idea how much of a b*tch I was back then, for lack of a better word. If I met my sixteen-year-old self now, I would probably want to beat my ass, too. Grant got kicked out of school for punching that window, and as soon as that happened, the entire student body turned against me. I had a target on my back. Shortly after that incident, I was awakened at 2:00 a.m. by someone punching me over and over and over in my stomach. He was just whaling on me. Before anyone could stop him he went running off into the darkness, and I never saw who it was. 😨 That's pretty eerie, right?

I hate to say it, but I deserved it. Grant was a very well-liked guy who had been there forever. My instigating a fight with Grant, for no reason other than jealousy, ended up getting him expelled. This was not going to end well for me. My parents, foreseeing this from conversations with staff, pulled me just before the school kicked me out. So first I had drowned in public school then I had almost gotten killed in private school. What was next for me?

Suicide thoughts

The first time the thought of killing myself ever entered my mind was in fourth grade. I had been arguing with my teachers so much that they moved my desk outside to work in the hall. I had been getting disciplined for arguing with increasing frequency. My brain has worked very hard to block out the specifics from my memory, but the arguments almost always stemmed from me having to follow rules that didn't make sense to me. As I sat out there facing the wall, I thought about my life. I thought about how I couldn't seem to make friends, I couldn't seem to get along with my teachers, and I couldn't get along with my family. I thought, "Maybe I don't want to live this life. Maybe I could kill myself." That might sound very disturbing to you, but in my mind I was just making a calculation. When I first told my parents I was thinking about killing myself, I didn't realize the seriousness of what I was saying. But when I saw their reactions, I realized the power that it had. I could either grumble about school, complain about not having friends, etc. or I could simply mention suicide, and finally people would understand how upset I really was. Saying I wanted to kill myself was an effective tool to make people sit up and pay attention to my complaints.

When I first started talking about suicide at ten, I was considering it as much as any autistic ten-year-old could consider such a thing. But pretty quickly an exchange with my parents led me to not seriously consider it ever again. In the midst of throwing a fit about God knows what, I reached for the suicide card. I said something to the effect of, "Don't come looking for me, I'll be up in Heaven." My mom said, "If you kill yourself, you won't be going to heaven!" This was a lightbulb moment for me, I don't even know if I believe in "Hell" but even if there is a .000001 percent chance of it, that's enough! I never truly considered committing suicide again after that. This is an example of how logical my mind is, versus most people's. Why didn't they just tell me that right from the start? Any logical calculation would show that nothing is worth the *mere possibility* of burning for eternity. Again, I don't even know if I believe in it, but *nothing* is worth that *chance,* and you could only reach a different conclusion by disregarding logic.

However, just because I never thought about acting on it, doesn't mean I never thought about it again. In my sophomore year of high school, when I was banging my head against the wall socially trying to fit in with a crowd of people who wanted nothing to do with me, I famously told my father "Don't be surprised if you come into my room tomorrow morning and see me hanging from the ceiling fan." (I'm not sure it's even possible to hang oneself on a ceiling fan, I think you might just kill the ceiling fan.) But this again, was me trying to send a message of how frustrated I felt. It's a message that, without attention-getting tactics like talking about suicide, can be pretty hard to convey.

As I write this, I have even thought recently about wishing I could die. My life is such a minefield of failures, no matter how hard I try. And I try really hard. I can't keep a job, I can't keep a girl, I can't keep a friend, I can't even keep track of my belongings for God's sake! Even with my perpetual optimism, everything in life tends to go wrong, more wrong than I ever thought it could. I feel like my optimistic nature is being slowly and painfully eroded by my increasingly soul-crushing life experiences.

The reason I don't kill myself is not just the Hell thing, it's also because I know it would hurt my family members. But what I do often wish is that someone would kill me or that I could just die through no fault of my own. When I hear on the news about someone dying in a tragic accident, sometimes I wish we could trade places. I wish I could somehow give them their life back if it meant giving up mine because frankly I'm sure they want to live more than I do.

Whenever someone is contemplating suicide, the response is automatically to prevent them from going through with it at all costs. But my question is, how come I have to do this life? I was brought into this world non-consensually; how come I don't get a say in whether I stay here? Sometimes it feels like I'm stuck at a house party where I don't like any of the people there, and I'm not being allowed to leave the party!

The worst part is the alienation. Looking back at my life, for the most part, I was never delusional. The problem was not what I didn't see, it was what I did see. Most people (in my opinion), don't perceive reality for everything it is. Or they do, and it doesn't bother them. With me it's a worst of both worlds thing, where I notice things other people don't notice, and I don't know how to not let it bother me. Like, in middle school, I knew being seen getting on the short bus would be bad news for me socially. Or in high school, I knew that succeeding with girls was a lot harder than people would have you believe. The issue is greatly exacerbated by my frustration when other people don't see what I see. So, when people give me advice, or try to tell me what I should do, they are coming from a different paradigm. A paradigm, frankly, I wish I could join them in. This is not me trying to brag about how smart I am because it's miserable seeing things on a different level from everybody else, especially when the sight is not pretty. Let me tell you, some knowledge is not worth having.

I know I'm supposed to leave you with some hope on this sunny chapter about suicide, but as of this writing, life has not given me hope to leave you with. If it weren't for the pain I know it would inflict on my family members or anxieties about the afterlife, I'm not sure I would still be here.

Asperger's Bootcamp—Winter-Spring 2008

In 2008 there were not many affordable options for difficult-to-handle teenagers with autism. My parents researched programs in Arizona and in Connecticut, but each was over $40,000 a year! My dad does okay, but I have three siblings. My parents could only reasonably afford to spend so much money on my schooling.

There was a school/program my parents had read about, called Zirconia Southern Journeys. Tell me how awesome this would sound if you were a teenager: it was an Asperger's "boot camp" in the wilderness of rural North Carolina. It had no TV, no Internet for students, no phones for students, nothing that connected us to the outside world at all. My parents knew that I would absolutely hate it there, so they were nice enough to not send me there before trying Mount Snow Academy. Now that everything had crashed and burned at Mount Snow Academy, they didn't have many places to turn.

Here is where it gets interesting. My parents planned something of a coup to get me out of New Hampshire and off to North Carolina. They unexpectedly showed up at Mount Snow Academy to whisk me away to North Carolina with no option given to me at all. As you can imagine, I didn't react to this too positively. People with autism hate sudden changes of plan that we have no control over. I was completely furious when they pulled into the house in New Hampshire. I lost it and refused to get in the car. I really didn't understand the magnitude of the trouble I had caused at Mount Snow Academy because I was literally just being myself. I had bought into the pop psychology that society religiously preaches, and now the result of me being myself was that I was standing outside a log cabin, meeting the much lower-functioning autistic kids I would be living with for the next four months.

Meanwhile, all I was trying to do was chase the rabbit! I had been determined to prove I could achieve some sort of normalcy as a teenager in high school. It might sound crass, but getting thrown into a wilderness camp with lower-functioning kids felt like I was an inner-city kid working hard trying to make it out of the hood, and now I had to go live at a homeless shelter. I felt like a colossal failure, and my feelings were justified.

Being at an Asperger's wilderness camp illuminated the reality of my issues. It is one thing to have unpleasant conversations with your school guidance counselor and to argue with your parents every night, but as long as you're still getting up at 6:00 a.m. and going to high school with everybody else, it doesn't feel like you're f*cking up that badly. I just knew I was arguing with people all the time and that not many people liked me. But when I was sent away to this radical situation, it drove things home for me in terms of perspective. Zirconia was just so off-the-beaten-path of most teenagers that it finally gave me an idea of how extreme my behavior had been.

While at Zirconia, we spent half the time on campus (a rustic summer camp converted into a school) and half the time in short buses traveling to remote areas of the South. Out in the wilderness, often along a river somewhere, we would have to do things like pitch tents, tie knots, find firewood and all that outdoorsy crap that I hate. I felt like I was a million miles from my AOL instant messenger and watching VH1. It was very much in the style of a boot camp with extremely rigid rules. For example, if you ate before everyone got their food, they made you leave the area where everyone else was sitting to eat alone in the woods and they would take away half your food. If you "talked back" (which the counselors could arbitrarily interpret as anything, depending on their mood), you could be forced to sleep outside, sometimes in the rain, in the mud, whatever the conditions.

They assigned everyone levels from one to four, based on how well you behaved and went with the program. To be promoted to the next level, you had to be pretty much perfect all week. Losing that status could happen as quickly as saying one wrong thing or annoying the counselors in any way. The reason we cared so much about the levels was because they all had perks. For example, if you were level two, you could go into a gas station to buy yourself a soda while on a trip. This was a big incentive to behave. We would get excited if we were allowed to drink something other than warm water. It was amazing how my priorities in life changed so drastically to where the highlight of my week was buying a root beer from a 7-11 to drink on a short bus.

When I was growing up, my family was never into camping. We were more a free-continental-breakfast-Hampton-Inn kind of family. I never thought I would be caught dead waking up in a sleeping bag covered in morning dew. Now you might be thinking that all the camping forced me to open my mind to new experiences, and to my surprise, I would actually find that I liked camping! *No.* If anything, it was more horrific than I even imagined. 😨 We didn't even sleep in tents. Nights in the wilderness were spent underneath a blue tarp that we had to tie between trees. Everyone on the staff was a huge outdoorsy person—they all lived for this crap. Christian Lander has a famous online blog, also published as a book, called *Stuff White People Like.* And on the list is, "Making you feel guilty for not going outside." As you just read that, I bet you laughed, because you know it's true. I feel like the entire organization of Zirconia Southern Journeys was founded on this very idea. The white counselors that worked there took it to another level. Not only did *they* live for the outdoors, *you* had to live for it, too. If you were anything short of absolutely mesmerized by Mother Nature, there was something wrong with you. The more experience I got being feasted on by mosquitoes, having every piece of clothing I owned get dirty, and sleeping with the rain coming through our tarps sideways, the less I appreciated it. (Hey, it could have been worse—at least it wasn't snowing!)

I complain a lot about the three semesters I spent at Zirconia, but as lame as it was with all the rules and all the outdoors, there was something about it I really liked. It was a small, quiet setting with the same group of around thirty people (staff *and* students) every day. There was a sense of comfort and safety that I still sometimes miss. The days were super-structured, life was predictable, and with all the colorful personalities of the students, we did have a lot of fun.

There were many inside jokes and hysterical moments. One of the kids was a boy named Riley who was literally around four hundred pounds. Every day he got in some kind of trouble, and every night he had to sleep outside. He constantly tried to get attention. He would pee in his sleeping bag, and as three or four counselors dragged him over to the hose the next morning he would wail and cry at the top of his lungs to try to get sympathy from everyone. If you don't laugh at this stuff, you'll cry!

Then there was Adam. Adam was a little bit lower-functioning, and he would take forty-five-minute showers and refuse to come out. Our showers had a fifteen-minute limit. The counselors would bust in to yank him out after his time was up. Usually they found him furiously rubbing himself on the bench in the shower. He had a unique personal style of masturbation. Later he started sneaking away from group during the day and the counselors would find him in the shower room having his way with the wooden bench. They had to physically remove him, as he would screech hysterically, "I need to masturbate! I need to masturbate!" We found out that his thing wasn't even girls or guys. Adam first got freaky with himself in a hotel room watching a documentary on dolphins. Dolphins were what did it for him. You have to admit, this is funny sh*t! For me and for some of the other guys there (and the counselors, even though they never admitted it), Zirconia was like watching an award-winning reality show.

This radio station helped me feel like I wasn't in the wilderness.

If one were to compare Zirconia to a 12-step program, the first step was admitting I had a problem. The second step was to understand exactly how I had been causing such a whirlwind of crises. As much as I hated having to be around a bunch of lower-functioning kids, they helped me gain a ton of self-awareness. They did this by showing me an exaggerated version of what my autism looked like. It was very uncomfortable, but very necessary.

I had always had a lot of trouble accepting answers I didn't like. It was especially challenging for me if the answer was "Yes," and then something changed, and the answer became "No." Food became what we all lived for at Zirconia. If the counselors were going to take us to McDonald's and then, because of a schedule change, we didn't get to go, one of the other kids wouldn't be able to accept the change. He would throw a fit and ask for the same explanation over and over, because he couldn't accept the unfortunate change in plans. This was an exaggerated version of the kind of behavior I knew all too well, because I did it myself. It sounds mean, but as soon as I saw the low-functioning kids pull antics like that, my desire to not be anything like them helped me improve my habits very quickly.

I stayed in North Carolina for four very long, phoneless, wilderness-filled months. Every time anything happened, I just thought to myself, "May 9th, you'll be outta here." I remember how I thought as soon as May hit, it would be so close, the last nine days would be a breeze. Unfortunately, like a forty-five-minute run on a treadmill, the closer the end got, the slower the time went. I was so anxious to be able to watch TV again and to get my Black-Berry back.

Anywhere you get a cold winter, springtime tends to bring a generally happy, upbeat mood with it. There was just something in the air those first few weeks back home from wilderness/autism camp: it seemed like good things were about to happen. I had taken my driver's license test twice and failed twice. The second time I tried to exit through a Do Not Enter sign and failed before we even left the parking lot. I had another chance to get my license right before summer began, and I would have been devastated if I had failed again.

For weeks I practiced driving with my parents and a profes-sional driving instructor. I couldn't mess this up. The third time *had* to be the charm. I still remember the words the examiner said after we finished the test, "Well, Dylan, you did good, you got a license." Sitting next to that examiner on the afternoon of May 28, 2008, if only I had known just how much impact this one moment would have on my life!

Summer 2008

When I got my driver's license in May 2008 the summer officially started. My car was a purple 1995 Volvo 850 station wagon, but like we all do with our first cars, I loved it because it was mine. Now, let me just say here, I knew it wasn't a coincidence that because I had a car, all of a sudden my phone was buzzing with plans. But I also knew that I believed in myself as a person. The way I looked at it was, if guys like Nick and all of his friends were spending time with me, they'd come to like me for more than just my car.

People tend to have this black and white idea of friendship: if someone is using you, they can't like you. It's either one or the other. My perspective was yeah, these guys might be calling me to hangout because I have a car, but they might also like me too. Friendship is not an on/off switch, it's a gradient. And hell, even if they were one hundred percent using me, being around them was opening up a whole world of social opportunities to me. Look, by 2008 I had been in a ten-year friendship drought, and I saw social interaction almost like food. If I'm starving, I'm not going to worry about *why* you're handing me a hamburger. I'm not going to ask, "Did you really *mean* to give me this hamburger?" No, when it came to social interactions in '08, my attitude was "I'm gonna eat!"

Having said all that, Nick and his crew seemed to genuinely find me hilarious. What was really crazy was I would have always thought of these guys as even cooler than the jocks, definitely way too cool for me to hang with. I had never for a second considered that the crowd I might fit in with would be, for lack of a better word, the badasses. Who would have thought they would be more accepting of me?

Me suddenly being the guy with the car was really incredible. Even before, when I briefly had friends here and there,

there was always this feeling that no matter what happened, the group would abandon me. We would be hanging out in a group I managed to finagle my way into, and like kids do, they would get distracted — "Something shiny!" — and then, for whatever reason (likely because I wasn't truly fitting into the group), they would walk away, totally forgetting about me. It happened all the time!

Now that I was the one who drove everybody there, and they all relied on me to make the next move, I was elevated to this position of power over the group. I loved it. And you could say, "Oh well, they were only staying around you because you had the car" — to which I would say, "Yeah, well, I only have a hard time being included because I have a disability." The car was social affirmative action. You could call my summer of 2008, "Dylan's summer of making up for lost time." That was not just in terms of friends, but it was also with girls. Nick's whole MO was basically, well, having sex with every girl he met. As a horny teenager, that fit perfectly with my agenda.

Nick was a tall, very good-looking blond guy. On top of that, his natural game with females was unreal. I didn't realize the magnitude of his skills until girl after girl would end up wanting him, and usually he wasn't even trying!

On the one hand I was glad to be rolling with this guy's crew — he was literally the coolest person I had ever met. On the other hand, it really bothered me when a girl I'd met and liked would just drop me for him. I hadn't developed much game at all back then, so it should not have surprised me, but it still got to me. When Nick and his friend Jay were talking to girls, I realized I was watching two pros play a game that I was a total rookie at. Then again on the positive side, I knew that even the fact that I was bringing these females around my new friends made me look great.

One night I was driving around Old Orchard Beach, Maine and Jay was riding shotgun, while Nick was in the backseat with a girl. I told you his MO. What I discovered was, that included while I was driving down a busy city street! One minute they're messing around heavy back there, and the next minute I look in the rearview mirror and see his bare ass pounding her up against the walls of my Volvo. 😫

I was totally inexperienced at handling social situations like this. I yelled at them to stop, even to the point where I wasn't watching the road. Jay grabbed the wheel, screaming, "Shut the f*ck up, just drive!!!"

There's no doubt that these guys weren't always nice to me and didn't respect me sometimes, but I wasn't the easiest guy to roll with back then. Even though I was, of course, always hilarious, I was unpredictable and often very inappropriate. These were guys that got invited to parties, guys that had friends from all over southern Maine, and guys that hung out with lots of very pretty girls. Most kids in my high school weren't willing to even be associated with me, so I was happy to have them as friends.

Nick, Jay, and two other friends I'd made, Mike and Alex, would freestyle (rap) to each other to see who had the sickest bars. One time Mike was sitting in the back while we were riding around, and he threw out, "His name is Dielawn, he spits like a lion . . . "

There it was: the moment Dielawn was born.

People sometimes have this idea that I cooked up a name and then went around begging everyone to call me it. I have Asperger's, but I ain't *that* socially retarded. Mike and Alex started using it, and from there it caught on with everyone else. I always thought that was pretty much the ideal path for a new nickname, right?

Friends that Are Girls

The summer of 2008 was such a milestone for me that looking back I see it in many ways as the beginning of my life as I know it. Everything is B.C. (Before Car) or A.C. (After Car). I spent the first half of that summer running around chasing girls, with either Nick and Jay, or Mike and Alex. I had finally made some male friends! But now . . . what about female friends?

On a late-July day in Old Orchard Beach, I met up with a girl I found on MySpace named Tiffany. When I picked her up, she was with her friend, Brittany, who had this really cool vibe about her; she seemed smart, very outgoing and confident, but not stuck-up. We only hung out for ten minutes, and then they had to get dropped off somewhere. As they were getting out of the car, I said, "Let's meet back up later," and something about the way Brittany replied, "Yeah, alright," made me think she might make a good friend. Sometimes you never forget those first impressions. Brittany actually had a boyfriend, but he rarely left his house, so she pretty much did whatever she wanted. To my surprise, Tiffany and Brittany wanted to hang out later. Brittany and I ended up becoming friends, and she introduced me to her friend Anna.

Anna didn't have a boyfriend, so naturally I tried really hard to get with her; why wouldn't I? She was tall and skinny with long blonde hair—I had to! I was asking her a few questions about herself, and then I used my classic line: "Wow, you're pretty badass—I think you might be a bad influence on me." But instead of flirting back, she looked confused and then just burst out laughing in my face. She wasn't having any of my game, but she thought my attempts at flirting with her were hilarious. She and Brittany basically said to me, "We're going to be friends and hang out every day." And that's exactly what happened.

I don't think I ever doubted from day one that the car was probably a big reason these girls were befriending me. But as I have already stated, I have no problem using incentives to get people in the door. Once you start hanging out, friendships can develop. Besides, even if they were totally using me for my car, I only wanted to be friends with them because they were cute, so doesn't it kind of go both ways? 😜

So Brittany, Anna, and I started hanging out all the time. I introduced them to Nick, Jay, Alex, and Mike, and now it was starting to feel like I had built a real social circle. It was like flying; I was over the moon! This was everything I had always wanted.

You may be wondering, "What did you guys do together, since they were girls? You couldn't go chasing girls like you did with the guys . . . " Oh yes, that's exactly what we did.

Anna and Brittany would go through their phones, trying to

get every girl they knew to hang out with us; the goal being to pick them up so I could try to hook up with them. I would tell them to "make me look good" and they knew exactly what I meant. They would brag about me and tell girls how cool I was, whatever it took to get them to hang with us. I wasn't sure if they were being genuine or if they were just appeasing me to get rides, but either way, how cool was that? I think on some level they knew that my desire to get girls wasn't coming from a malicious "use them and lose them" mindset. On a much deeper level, I wanted the validation of female approval, and I think Anna and Brittany knew that. If not, then they were really good actresses! We would be at my house with a girl they had convinced to hang out with us, and they would make up an excuse to leave the room so I could be alone with her. They'd stay in the next room, listening to me talk to her; then they'd pull me aside to give me pointers on what to do and what not to do—like, "Here, take some gum so you have fresh breath—put your collar like this—don't wear your shirt like that—don't say that, go back in there and say this!" As it was happening, I was thinking, "This is adorable—it's like we're inside a movie."

Brittany was really the perfect candidate for a friend. She came from a pretty normal family, but Maine has this unique situation where parents can really not give a f*ck about what their kids do; because it's Maine, they can be out all hours of the night, and nothing bad is really going to happen to them. Brittany would be out for days—she would stay at Anna's, or once when my parents went away for the weekend, both Brittany and Anna stayed with me and slept in my sister's room. In the morning I woke up, and Brittany was in my room on my computer talking to people and trying to set up things for us to do; it was pretty surreal. A year before then, if you had told me that I would have a car and two female friends who would stay with me for the weekend and spend their time chasing girls with me, I don't know what I would have said.

You may be asking why two girls would put in all this effort to help me get with their friends. A couple of years later, when Brittany was seventeen, she ended up starting a family with a guy she met back when we were hanging out. (I actually felt kind of bad because when they first started dating, I told her she shouldn't date him because he seemed like a douchebag; turns out I was wrong.) But seeing how thrilled she was to be a mother put our friendship in perspective. It clicked with me that it had been Brittany's mothering instincts that were the driving force of our friendship. I think she saw me as this guy who had potential but needed some guidance, almost like a project. Even though I was older than she, I was like a proxy for her to be this mother-like figure to before she had kids of her own. That's my theory anyway, and I think I'm right. 😉

Anna was a different story. With her I think we just bonded personality-wise. Everyone claims to have a great sense of humor, but in my opinion few people actually do, and Anna was one of those people. She laughed at things I said when I wasn't even trying to be funny; she was very sarcastic, and she could make me laugh, too. As we know, I can be pretty hard to talk to sometimes, but once in a while I run across someone who seems to be on the same wavelength as me. When I'm frustrated or when I'm not understanding something, it's like they know what I'm thinking. Anna was one of those people who could break things down for me and explain them so that I understood. If I found myself in arguments with people (as I often did) or if I didn't understand what was going on, she would interrupt and be like, "Oh my god, Dielawn, this is what they're saying!" or "This is what it means!" and she'd spell it out for me in a way that always made sense.

I was still very self-conscious about my disability back then, I didn't want anyone to know I had Asperger's. Nick's parents had known my parents for a long time, so he knew about it, and I found out one day that pretty much everyone else knew, too. I was texting Anna, who told me she had heard about it, and I was all upset and pretty much sperging out about people knowing.

She said, "It doesn't affect how I see you or how I think of you at all." I felt like she knew exactly how to get through to me. I don't know if she felt the same way, but for me it was a really cool bond.

Anna had a whole group of girls in Old Orchard Beach that

she introduced me to, and they all became my friends. I found that girls in OOB were much more accepting than the girls I went to school with in Sedgefield, where the culture was, "If you don't play sports, you don't exist." These girls all came from sketchier circumstances than Sedgefield girls (one of their mothers even bought them cigarettes and alcohol). But I felt much more comfortable being friends with girls who hadn't had perfect lives, even if their obstacles were very different from mine.

I said my goodbyes to everyone in September and went back to Asperger's boot camp in North Carolina. When I came home for a few weeks during winter break in December 2008, I was worried they had all forgotten about me, and the break wouldn't live up to the whirlwind summer I'd had. But it was just the opposite: that break was like the entire summer condensed into three weeks. The first day I was back, I hit up Nick and Jay. I went to Jay's house in Gorham—it was snowing, and they ran up to me in the snow, screaming, "Dielawn!" and ripped off my hat, it felt great! While over the summer I had hung out more with Brittany, during that break I started to get really close to Anna, who lived a lot nearer. I'm sure you're already predicting what happened next. I should have known I was going to develop feelings for Anna: she really was everything I had always looked for in a girl, looks-wise and personality-wise; it was only a matter of time. She was a total badass. Anna really embraced the whole party-girl image: drinking, smoking, and making out with her girlfriends—she was like a real-life Ke$ha! You know how some girls are attracted to bad boys? I'm attracted to bad girls. I feel nothing for good girls who follow all the rules. I liked that Anna didn't take herself too seriously, and she wasn't stuck-up. But what really got me was that underneath it all, she was actually really smart; that, to me, was the coolest thing about her.

During the break Anna hit me up almost every day, and she was down to tag along for whatever I wanted to do. I spent the break riding around with all the same friends from the summer, Jay, Nick, Mike, and Alex. But no matter what we did, I insisted we had to go pick up Anna. She was like my sidekick, and I always wanted her around. I didn't realize I might be getting too attached to her until one night in January, right before I left to go back to North Carolina. It was Anna's birthday, and I found out she had done some stuff with Nick. I shouldn't have been surprised, because literally every girl wanted Nick, but it really got to me, and I just couldn't stand the thought that she had gotten with one of my friends and not with me. Alex noticed I was upset and spoke out on my behalf: in front of everyone, he said to Anna, "Do you not see what's going on here? Every day I've been with him, it's 'let's go pickup Anna, let's hang out with Anna!' He obviously likes you!"

Luckily, I was eventually able to get over those feelings for Anna. But for a while I got really hung up on the fact that my other friends, especially Nick and Jay, were able to hook up with girls that I was just friends with. I thought I should be able to be "friends with benefits" like they were, and if I couldn't be on their level, there must be something wrong with me. Unfortunately, I didn't have enough validation back then from other girls to know that I don't have to get with every single girl.

I really wish I had appreciated my friendships with Brittany and Anna instead of worrying about what they were doing with another guy friend. I found out much later that Anna and Brittany were very much another example in my life of "save the best for first." Female friends like them are not a dime a dozen, especially ones who would be as patient with me as Anna and Brittany were, let alone trying to set me up with other girls, telling them good things about me. The friendship just happened so easily that I didn't realize what I had.

One myth portrayed by Hollywood that really annoys me is this idea that dorky, lame guys just happen to get friend-zoned by knockout, gorgeous women. That's bullsh*t. Beautiful women have many, many guys who would love to settle for being best friends with them. To genuinely become close friends with a hot girl is just about as difficult as dating her; I know this because I have since succeeded a few times. Girls don't just friend-zone any Steve Urkel—the guy has to be on roughly the same level as someone they would date. Water seeks its own level, and that applies to friendship too.

Another mistake I made back then, was being very demanding of everyone in order to avoid being taken advantage of. I was vaguely aware that some of my new friendships might be, to varying degrees, because I had a car and they didn't. But I had a very hard time being able to effectively identify who was a real friend, who was using me for my car, and who was anywhere in between. The way I coped with this was by overcompensating: I demanded that people either give me gas money everywhere we went or introduce me to girls. My overcompensating to avoid being used probably turned into a self-fulfilling prophecy. As a matter of fact, I know it did. I wish I hadn't been so demanding, but what was the alternative? I had no idea how to read people. I had no idea how to spot clues of people's intentions. I had no idea who was real and who was fake. If I could go back and relive those years now, it would be like my eyes were opened, the blinders taken off. But back then I just didn't know how to be chill when I was so unsure of everything and everyone.

How Do You Get Fired from McDonald's?

In the spring of 2008, I got a job at the local McDonald's. Before summer even started, my parents had been on me about getting a summer job. My mom kept pushing me to apply at Shaw's, a local grocery store, because she knew someone that worked there, and Shaw's was known for being flexible with hours. Working at Shaw's also meant that I would be able to resume that job whenever I was home during the summer. Naturally, I did not want that job, mostly because it was my mom's idea.

I only applied to a couple of places before I got an interview at McDonald's. I was very proud of myself and thought that was a huge accomplishment. The McDonald's owners, Rick and Leanne, were a married couple who were extremely nice. They really liked me, and I had a great interview. At the time, I didn't know that

McDonald's would basically hire you if you could breathe, so in my mind, this was a huge win. I told my parents about it, and they were against the idea of me working at McDonald's. So, of course, I took the job.

Some of the McDonald's employees were Sedgefield High School students that I thought were pretty cool. They let me bring my radio to work and allowed me to put on the local hip-hop station (yes, Maine had one of those). Not long after I started the job, we were listening to my music, and the song "Dangerous" by Akon (actually by Kardinal Offishall, but nobody remembers him) came on. I suddenly started doing this wild dance to it like I was having a seizure. Everyone thought I was hilarious, and it immediately became my thing. All of a sudden, I was popular with everyone at work, almost like an exact reproduction of the Disney cruise I talked about before.

I didn't think it could last though. This was a fun job but also very challenging and extremely fast-paced, with a lot of multi-tasking. My shifts often began at 7:00 a.m. For me, waking up at 6:00 a.m. was *not* the way I wanted to spend my summer. I was a good sport, and I did it, but I was far from learning how to keep a job.

Before long, the mistakes started happening. A few times, I gave a customer the wrong order, and once I undercooked a piece of meat and gave it to a customer. The mistake that got me fired was messing up the timer on the fryer. Instead of asking for help, I just eyeballed the meat, and it looked cooked to me, so I went ahead and served it. Apparently that was a big no-no in food service, and when the customer complained that her meat was undercooked, that was it for me. This was just two weeks after I debuted my seizure dance. When Leanne, Rick, and the assistant manager sat me down and told me that they had to let me go, the assistant manager was literally on the verge of tears. That made it feel not so bad!

Two weeks before summer ended and I went back to North Carolina, I got a job at Dunkin' Donuts. This was one of the only jobs I didn't get fired from, but that's because I was leaving in two weeks. Given more time, no doubt it would have been added to the list.

An Entire Summer in Three Weeks

At this time of my life, my mood had gone from defeated to on top of the world—maybe a little overconfident. Maine can be rough in the winter. One day in January 2009, we had a huge snowstorm. It's funny, when your life is going so great and it's filled with friends, adventures, new experiences and excitement, you don't care how cold and dark it is outside. I went up to Belgrade, Maine, to see a girl I had met online. Belgrade is very much in the middle of nowhere, and how I found a half-black girl in Belgrade, Maine, I'll never know.

It was rural open country with giant hills. I was driving my mom's Yukon XL, and feeling like I was the *sh*t*. I was also driving faster than I should have been for the weather conditions, and I wasn't being careful. Suddenly, the car went out of control and I veered off into a snowbank. Even then my mood wasn't broken. I felt like, "I got this. I'm going to get out of it."

Meanwhile, I had never had a car stuck in snow before, so I had no idea what to do. My parents didn't know that I had gone an hour-and-a-half away from Sedgefield to hook up with some chick. It was the day before I was going to go back to Zirconia, the boarding school in North Carolina, for four months. I would have four months when I couldn't even have a cellphone, much less hook up with a chick—so I was *not* going to let the evening go to waste.

There I was stuck in the snow, and I couldn't call my parents for help. This was a bad situation. I could see a house like a mile away, and the girl's house like a half-mile behind it. I was in my mom's Yukon XL, stuck in a snowbank in Belgrade, Maine, and the sun was setting. I promise that I couldn't make this up, but it turned out there was a house through the woods exactly where I was stuck. Out of nowhere, a man in a pickup truck, this guardian angel-like figure, emerged from the forest with tow gear. He got me out of the snowbank in less than five minutes—just hooked the car up and yanked it out. I was good to go, and it was the best day ever! It worked out, and my parents (until they read this book) never heard the story. Sorry, Mom and Dad.

Back in high school, if I can be honest, the best part of getting laid (besides getting laid) was telling everybody that you got laid. Sometimes telling everyone the next day was even better. Before I left Belgrade, I got on my phone and I texted *everybody* I knew, all in caps, "GUESS WHAT . . ."

When I think about all that went down right before I got sent back to boarding school, it really does feel like it was a movie, or at least a really good book *wink*. That may sound like bragging, but for someone who had no friends and absolutely no social life for so many years that was what it felt like. Anna and all her girlfriends made me a card the night I was leaving where they wrote "We Love You Dielawn!" and on the inside they wrote down a list of all our inside jokes. When I got to Zirconia I taped it on my cubby so I could look at it every day (and show it off to all the counselors). Wow, what good times—can it be January 2009 again? 😜

My last night in Maine was truly special. I know that things probably would not have stayed that great if I hadn't left Maine for boarding school. My life doesn't ever stay good for long. As good as it gets is as hard as it crashes.

I will admit that the entire Christmas break wasn't completely a whirlwind of perfection. I have a habit of remembering just the good things in life. It's a great coping mechanism, given all the crap I've been through. One night during my time home, I got an AOL instant message from my friend Mike. He asked me if I could sneak out with my parents' car after they went to bed to take him to the store to buy a pack of cigs. It would have been way past my curfew, which was midnight at that time.

My parents had installed software that allowed them to monitor all my conversations. My mom usually didn't read them, but there was always a chance she would because they all got sent to her email. It was very much every teenager's worst nightmare. I told Mike that I couldn't sneak out and then wrote some self-righteous crap, but immediately afterward I called him and explained that I had to say that because my parents read my conversations, but I would do it. Mike was a badass, break-the-rules type kid, but he was also intelligent. He understood what was up, and twenty minutes later, he messaged me, "So what was said, is that still in effect?" I don't know why, but I still find that hilarious.

At 2:00 a.m., after I knew my parents were asleep, I went to pick him up. Of course I wanted to seem cool by coming through like this for him, but I also looked at every social situation as an opportunity that I didn't want to miss. It's unfortunate, and I do feel bad looking back, that I prioritized my social life way above respecting my parents. They didn't deserve that. But that's just the way I was in my high school years. I was definitely a brat.

I was feeling pretty dangerous escaping my house at 2:00 a.m. I started speeding, because there is nobody on the roads in Maine at 2:00 in the morning. For some reason, I assumed that the cops weren't around either. I was driving at least twenty miles an hour over the speed limit, and I even ran a red light. Again, I don't know what I was thinking. Why couldn't I just be happy that I got away with sneaking out? As always with me, I just had to push it further.

Mike said, "Slow down, you're gonna get pulled over!" I didn't listen to him. I kept driving really fast. Next thing I knew Mike says, "Slow down, Dielawn, you got a cop behind you!" This was the first time that I had ever been pulled over—in the middle of the night, when I was supposed to be home in bed. I knew I was screwed. I started flipping out, asking Mike if they would take my license away.

"Does this mean I won't be able to drive for the next couple weeks?"

"Does my license get taken away immediately or when I go to court?"

"What happens if I go away and they know I'm not driving while I'm at boarding school? Will they wait to take my license away when I come back to Maine and I have my car again?"

I was in a state of panic, like a very I-want-my-mommy kind of mentality. Mike said, "Dude, stop asking me f*cking twenty questions, I don't know."

The cop gave me a ticket for running a red light. I didn't tell my parents until the day before I left to go back to boarding school. I'd love to say that I did the right thing and told them as soon as it happened, but that would have meant that the amazing three weeks I had over break never would have happened.

When everything was said and done, I had to lose my license for only thirty days. I was going to boarding school in North Carolina where I couldn't drive anyway, so it basically meant there was no punishment at all.

My very kind parents surprisingly understood, because they knew I was making up for lost time for all those years when I had no friends. I really got away with that one. If you're reading this and feel that I shouldn't have gotten away with it, don't worry—if you keep reading, you'll read about plenty of times I totally got nailed. Trust me, I don't get away with a lot of things, but in this case I made out pretty well.

Quaint Troubles

Nick and I were seventeen but Jay was only fifteen. Jay loved to drive though, and this kid knew how to drive like nobody's business. My thinking back then, which was probably true, was that he was a better driver than I was. My driving was kind of brutal in those early days of having my license—I made a lot of mistakes and got distracted easily. I had miraculously gotten my license after a couple of driving test failures, but I still had some lessons to learn on the road.

I had been letting Jay drive all summer even though it was illegal, because he only had his permit and I wasn't eighteen. In fact, he wasn't even technically allowed to be in the car when I drove under Maine law!

Jay was driving through Old Orchard Beach one nice summer day when he and Nick got into an argument. Nick put down the window and started screaming, "WE GOT A FIFTEEN-YEAR-OLD DRIVER HERE! FIFTEEN-YEAR-OLD DRIVER!!"

Jay always had such an attitude like he was hot sh*t, so it was funny to see him actually get upset as he yelled, "Shut the f*ck up, dude. SHUT. THE. F*CK. UP!!!"

But Nick didn't care about anyone except Nick, so he kept yelling, "HEY, FIFTEEN-YEAR-OLD UNLICENSED DRIVER IN THIS CAR!" Luckily, it was the middle of the summer with a million people around the beach, so no one paid any attention. It was another one of those moments where I almost wanted to pinch myself, because a year earlier, during that miserable summer of 2007, I never thought I would be riding around with guys who were alpha enough to do wild and crazy sh*t like that, and that I would actually be included in on the joke. I couldn't believe I had gone from zero to a hundred this quick. (Drake reference)

Another day I got a text in all caps from my dad. It said, "JAY'S MOM JUST SAW JAY DRIVING!" This was the first time I had really been in trouble with my parents. My dad was pissed!

When I look back on the much more serious things I've been in trouble for since then, it seems like a quaint time. My parents probably feel the same way. But at that time, I had an awful feeling in the pit of my gut, my stomach was doing flips, and my heart sank. And this wasn't even my car, I was using my mom's Yukon XL that day. I didn't want to go home.

We went to the Sedgefield High School parking lot and hung out. We were all smoking cigs outside the car. I made them smoke outside the car only because I had just received that angry text, and I knew I was already in big trouble. I wanted to air out the car, because I had been letting everyone smoke in it, which was obviously strictly forbidden by my parents.

When you're with a bunch of fifteen- and sixteen-year-olds who love to smoke and it's twenty degrees outside, it's very hard to be the stickler who pulls over and makes everyone get out of the car every single time they want to light up. No matter how inconsiderate it was to let people smoke in my mom's car, it would have cost me socially if I didn't. And you can say "Oh well, they must not have been *real* friends if they couldn't respect your wishes," but you're thinking about it backwards. Try to think back to being a teenager—being the guy who enforces unpopular rules is what causes you to *lose* respect. BREAKING NEWS: Teenagers are not mature. Not everyone, especially the group I hung out with, was raised well—and most teenagers, unless they were raised by a *really* upstanding family, will see you as a wet blanket if you insist on pulling over and having everyone go outside in the middle of the winter every time they want to blaze a cig. That's just a fact! So, I'm not proud of it, but I did let people smoke in her car. I thought I could disguise it by bringing it home at night and leaving the windows down while she slept. It rarely worked. As soon as my mom got in the car she would get angry and accuse me of letting people smoke in her car. I would always aggressively deny it and say they all smoke, so they smell like cigarettes, and that's why her car smelled. She probably didn't believe me, but I thought I was convincing, and she couldn't prove that I was lying. (Little did my parents know I had actually started smoking cigarettes, too—a habit I would wrestle with for years to come.)

I thought this day would be no different until I got that text from my very angry dad. All of a sudden, I was sh*tting myself. I knew when I got home there would be hell to pay and, I suspected, some kind of discipline. I was terrified of losing my permission to drive. Meanwhile, Jay's mom wasn't even going to be mad at him. Jay's mom was more like his best friend than his parent. Believe it or not, she was mad at my parents and at me. I'm not even sure why. As much as I was not happy that my parents were going to come down on me like a ton of bricks, situations like that reminded me that I had a good upbringing.

There I was, standing in the school parking lot, miserably thinking, "What the hell is going to happen to me?"—trying to buy some extra time so the car could air out and my dad could maybe cool down. When I got home, my parents asked me why I let Jay drive the car. I said, "Well, he *is* a better driver than I am. Most people are better drivers than I am. Whenever someone's willing to drive, I let them, because we're all safer than when I'm driving.

"So, if you think about it that way, you should actually be

thanking me for being so responsible."

I don't know where I came up with that bullsh*t, but as I said it, we all realized that it actually made some sense. I lost car privileges only for a weekend, and we all look back at that story and laugh at my unique logic for breaking the rules.

Meeting Mark (kind of)

Pop music has always been my default special interest, and it started really re-emerging in 2009. I began closely following the music charts again and found a forum online that would become a staple in my favorites. On the "Pulse Music Boards" forum other chart geeks would discuss every single song that got released and have intellectual debates about each song's performance on the charts, music in general, and everything I loved to obsess over. It was my special interest, and now there was actually an online forum for me to connect with.

I had never met or even heard of anyone who talked about pop music the way I like to—literally not one person. I love to intellectualize it. I meticulously study the trends, paying attention to how music has evolved. I analyze what was hot a year ago, what was hot five years ago, and I think about why. I look at how songs sound different now than they did a few years ago. I try to figure out why some songs are a hit while other songs are a flop. But I realized early in my life that finding somebody else to talk with about these things was a pipe dream. It's remarkable really. I have seen neurotypical people get into impassioned conversations about different kinds of soil for growing potatoes, but the second pop music is brought up, the room goes silent.

When I got on the forums, I discovered they mostly consisted of gay guys who wanted to follow the careers of their favorite divas. But I didn't care, I was just glad to know I wasn't the only one who wanted to talk about whether Rihanna released the right single. I ended up connecting with one person who ended up being one of the longest, most consistent friends I have ever had.

Mark was a hip-hop music producer from D.C. We first bonded

over being the only two straight guys on the forum. We started texting about anything and everything happening in the world of Top 40 and Urban radio. We'd even talk on the phone for hours and never run out of things to say. Meeting Mark online was like hitting the friendship jackpot! He was the first person I ever met who looked at music in the deep analytical way that I did. He was pretty much in the same boat as I was, with none of his friends on the same level either. And no, he didn't have Asperger's, if that's what you're thinking. That is what my parents assumed when they heard me talking about him. 😂

Talking to Mark educated me about quite a few things, like the difference between Atlanta hip-hop and New York hip-hop and, since he happened to be black, everything I ever wanted to know about black culture. To this day, he is the only person I have ever known who could point stuff out to me about music that had me like, "Damn, I never thought about that." And I'm the walking pop music encyclopedia! 😨

One time my mom saw a text on my phone come in from Mark that read "Have you heard Usher's new song 'OMG'? It's straight electro-pop, and Will.i.Am's verse has a LOT of auto-tune." and she said to my dad, "Honey, I think someone is after our son's heart."

Mark and I don't talk as often as we used to, but if we could finally meet maybe that would revive our friendship. If you are in Washington, D.C., and happen to book speaking engagements, bring me there for a gig, and when Mark and I hang out I'll be sure to send you a picture!

Chili's

When I was a senior in high school, my parents and I agreed that I needed a part-time job. I applied and got hired as a host at a local Chili's restaurant. It was the perfect job for me. I got to work with some cute girls, the job wasn't too hard, and I met a lot of interesting people. I loved it! I wanted to keep everything ethical and above-board, so after I was offered the job, but before I completed all the paperwork, I brought my dad in to meet my boss and help me explain my disability.

One of most important lessons I have learned as a person with high-functioning autism is that I cannot understate my disability, or people will most definitely underestimate the impact that it has on my life in every way. The meeting went great, as my boss explained that she, too, had a child on the spectrum. I don't always believe people when they tell me that they have a relative with autism. It seems like it's sort of the "cool" thing to say, like white people claiming to have black friends or straight people claiming to have gay friends. With the amount of people who have told me they have a family member with autism, mathematically it's just not possible they're all telling the truth! But I took her word for it, maybe she was telling the truth. My new boss assured my dad and me that she could and would be totally accommodating and very direct in communicating exactly what was expected of me. It all sounded like this job was going to work out great—nothing to worry about here.

The problem is that when you don't appear as if you have a disability, people underestimate its impact, time and time again. They think, "Well, he's really smart . . ." Even if they know intellectually that someone has a disability, if it doesn't *seem* like they do, oftentimes that's all that matters.

I was able to keep the job at Chili's for about a month. Four weeks seemed to be the most common length of time before the axe would fall. It would and still does usually go like this: during the first week, they couldn't fire me because they had just hired me—they think I'll be fine once I'm trained. The second week, I'm still pretty new to the job, so they want it to work out. The third week they're starting to think, "Uh-oh, is this guy going to make it?" It's also at about three weeks that they forget about my disability and start going by what they feel—and what they feel is that they're getting sick of me. By the fourth week, they've had it with me. They're done with the constant instructions that I need, and they're annoyed by some of the decisions I've made or things

I have said, so I get fired. That's how it happened on this job, and would become the pattern for future employment to this day.

Here is a perfect example to illustrate what I'm describing. The first strike occurred when I was assigned to work under a long-time female worker who had been there over a year and had even been Employee of the Month. I trusted her to give me guidance. One evening, she and I were joking around prior to the arrival of a family with a very cute daughter. I was feeling more comfortable in showing my personality, which is my normal progression of behavior at jobs. I enjoyed making my coworkers laugh and I hadn't caused any problems up to this point. I asked my supervisor if I could seat them and told her, "That girl is really hot." So, my heretofore "trustworthy" supervisor said, "You should go slip her a note. Write your number on it, fold it up, and give it to her as she leaves. It would be funny."

I said, "No. I shouldn't do that, should I?" She insisted, "Yeah, do it!"—this was coming from Ms. Employee of the Month, who was totally neurotypical, and someone I should have been able to trust. I have a tendency to look at neurotypical people's advice like they're God, and it's the word of the gospel. Also, beneath many of my blunders in life, there is a grain of truth. And the truth is that different workplaces have different atmospheres, in which different things are considered acceptable—that *is* true! Chili's was what would be considered a laid-back work atmosphere, so maybe people would think it was a funny bit!

Never one to back down from a dare, I did it. I wrote my number down next to "Text me," with a backward smiley face. I folded it up and, as the family was leaving, I handed it to the girl with a smooth, "Hey, you forgot this." In a fun plot twist, the girl turned out to be fourteen! To make matters worse, the family was visiting from out of town, and their motel room at the Days Inn was literally in the Chili's parking lot. In no time, in marched her dad—not in the greatest of moods—and you can imagine the "formal complaint" he lodged! Luckily, I wasn't the only one who got in trouble. The female host and I both received write-ups.

Then, a few weeks later, a mandatory meeting was called for all employees at Chili's. I was never verbally informed of the meeting, but there was a notice on the bulletin board which, apparently, I was supposed to know I should be checking regularly. Amid a number of other notices and legally required posters, there was a sheet of paper announcing the mandatory company meeting on Saturday morning at 7:30 a.m. It said, in very clear and unmistakable fashion, "Mandatory"—big words, underlined, and in large print. Unfortunately, individuals with Asperger's have difficulty with clutter, especially in my case. I can't think straight if there's clutter. It becomes white noise, and I have a very hard time sorting through it. And the more clutter there is, the harder it is for my brain to take it in and process it.

Remember, when she met with my dad and me, my boss said she would be very clear and very direct with me. What she should have said was, "If you don't check this bulletin board regularly, there could be something on there that you miss, and that could result in your getting fired." That would have been clear and direct. It would have driven it home for me. But nothing was said to me, so I was home asleep during the "mandatory" meeting.

That would have been only two strikes, but of course, I had overslept and missed a shift too.

These three-strike systems common in workplaces are devised by and for neurotypical people, for whom three screw-ups is reasonable to avoid. The oversleeping and missing a shift—that's not a mistake I can blame on my disability. That was just a mistake like many people would make. And for most people it would have just been that one. The thing with me is I make those regular mistakes AND the ones because of my disability. So three strikes come nice and fast.

The Sisters

I do indeed have three younger sisters: Mariah (upper right) was born in 1994, Lilly (left) in 1998, and Serena (lower right) in 2004. I was established in 1991 so yes, I am the oldest. People always respond with a tiresome, "Oh wow!" when I tell them that. I am not sure if they are surprised I have three sisters or that I am the oldest. I do think it's unfortunate that I was born before all of them, because something about me doesn't fit the role of the oldest sibling.

Some people mature faster than others, and some mature slower. My maturity level has always significantly lagged behind my age, whereas Mariah has always been mature for her age. I have often wished she was my older sister, that way the situation where she often takes a leading role among the four of us would be much more natural. If you think of life as a forest that we are hiking through, it would be nice to have another sibling to look to ahead of me on the path, instead of me being up front, looking back at my three sisters following. The dynamic doesn't fit us; frankly, I wouldn't mind if they were all older than I am.

At speaking events, people are always dying to know about the relationship between my sisters and me, but I never feel like there is much to tell. I like to think we have a relatively normal relationship. They have always been good at bonding with me over things we all like.

All of us share a similar, very quirky sense of humor and my sisters have always thought I was funny. In fact, they were always my biggest fans. They were always there to cheer me on in my social endeavors as well. If I brought a girl home, they would be the first to high-five me and say, "She was pretty!" which I know they didn't think every time, but it was what I wanted to hear. 🙂

Since Mariah and I are closest in age, we watched TV together growing up. When we were little, we loved *Arthur* on PBS. As we got older, our favorite show became *The Office*. If you are familiar with *The Office,* you might agree that the jokes on that show fall into two categories—there's the broad humor that everyone gets (like Michael driving his car into a lake), and then there's all this subtle, weird stuff in there that only some people appreciate. Mariah and I would always be laughing over the weird stuff, reciting entire scenes word for word. Unfortunately, her taste in music is mostly acoustic and Christian rock, which is about as far from what I like as you can get. Luckily there is some overlap in pop music that we both like, and she's smart, so she has always known that music is how to bond with me.

Lilly and I have had a harder time bonding because we have less in common. Her taste in music is very different from mine, but in a way, it's exactly the same. She likes to listen to many really masculine sounding guy singers because that is the type of guy she's attracted to. It's kind of the mirror image of me—I like listening to really b*tchy-sounding female singers, and she was the first person to point that out to me. I was impressed! It kind of blew my mind when I thought about it. I definitely believe that most people enjoy listening to singers whom they would be most attracted to in person. One other cool thing about Lilly is she's *woke* when it comes to girls. Anytime I have some situation I'm dealing with or a complaint about girls, she never tries to gaslight me or give me cliché advice. She keeps it real.

Back in 2012, there was an incident when I was being really

obnoxious, and Lilly had been hitting me out of frustration. After she hit me the third time, since I couldn't hit her back, I actually used pepper spray on her. I was a train wreck at that time, but obviously there's no defending using pepper spray on your own sister. Yeah, she was hitting me pretty hard, but then again, I was being pretty obnoxious. I am not sure if our relationship was permanently scarred because of that, but I'm sure it didn't help.

B*tchy-sounding female vocalists may be my favorite, but I do like to listen to rap music sometimes too. Mariah and Lilly never liked rap, so I had kind of given up on being able to listen to any of that stuff with my sisters. But when Serena, the youngest, was ten or eleven, I realized maybe I have a sister with my taste in music after all! We also like to watch a show called *The Rap Game* together. *The Rap Game* is a reality show where five young rap kids compete for a record deal. Ironically, other than that TV show, we both share a dislike for children. Mariah was always very academically-focused in school; Lilly was super-popular with the sports crowd; and so far I would say Serena is the badass sister. Serena just has certain sensibilities that are similar to mine that Mariah and Lilly don't have. She's very alpha-female; her best friend is a girl who's two years older than her.

When I was younger, I put our family through a lot. I was a highly problematic child who argued viciously with my parents on a very regular basis, regularly disrupting my sisters' lives. Remarkably, they don't seem to hold any ill-will toward me over those years.

The challenging side of things for me, is watching as my sisters lead lives that are relatively free of any obstacles. It's frustrating when I tell people this, because they immediately want to countersignal me and say, "Well, I'm sure that's not true." —*what makes you so sure about that?*

Look, nobody's perfect, but some people are a hell of a lot closer than others. Maybe I'm biased, but my sisters seem as close to perfect as you can get. They aren't just regular girls with normal lives. They honestly have these cartoonishly overachieving lives in which not only does almost everything go right for them, they even succeed above and beyond most people. They excel in sports, they get straight A's in school, they are popular, and have rarely spent any time outside of a serious and healthy relationship with a man of their dreams. Meanwhile I couldn't make it through college, I can't keep a job, and I can barely manage to get a second date with a girl.

I try to be happy for them, but every time I hear news of their latest extraordinary accomplishments, it's hard not to feel that it's being rubbed in my face in the most extravagant fashion—what my life might be like without the autism. It's fair to look to an average, if you will, of the lives of all my family members, and if I didn't have autism, I'd say it's almost certain my life would be very comparable.

I used to believe my autism might someday make me even more successful as an adult, because of the special skills Asperger's comes with (memorizing facts, being hyper-focused on one thing, etc.) But I think I've been guilty of the same mistake other people make in assessing me. I think looking in the mirror, my own presentation skills have fooled me into not realizing how real my disability is. The way that my sisters continuously overachieve even compared to their peers, is the way I continue to cartoonishly fail in all of my life's endeavors. I often fail in ways that are so over-the-top it's almost comical, as you'll see reading the rest of this book.

The more I contrast my life's experiences with the experiences of my sisters, the more I am coming to understand the extent of my own disability. It's unfortunate that we have to lead such dissimilar paths, but despite how it may sound, I try not to let any of these things influence the way I think of or treat my sisters. It's not their fault that they are so nearly perfect, what are they supposed to do? They have always been as supportive of me as they can be, and that's all you can ask for.

"Flawda"

College Try #1: Palm Beach Community College, Fall 2010

In the fall of 2010 my parents had signed me up for a program we will call New Pathways that was designed to help people with autism navigate their way through college. I enrolled at Palm Beach Community College having been told by my high school that I was capable of college-level work.

I had been in special ed math for years and hadn't taken a grade-level math class since fourth grade. I dreaded taking a college-level math class, and it was worse than I could have ever imagined. I have a *very* low spatial IQ; math is just painful to my brain. It didn't make it any better that the teacher didn't like me. On one occasion I had gone to class forgotting to bring notetaking materials. Because it's easier for me to concentrate, I was conveniently sitting right up front. When the teacher told me I should be writing something down, I started writing it on my hand. As you can imagine, she pounced on this opportunity to lambaste me in front of the whole class. A neurotypical person would probably have avoided all three of these mistakes: forgetting the materials, sitting up front, and then writing on my hand. But I have no such foresight. Regardless of all that, I really did want to get through these courses and be successful. What I learned quickly is that I am not cut out for college—even community college. I have no ability to organize my time. I have no skills at multi-tasking. I can't take notes, (even when I remember my materials) because with autism, I can't distinguish between what I should write down (because I'll be tested on it) and what's just superfluous information. To me, it seems like everything the teacher says and every word in the book has equal importance.

Lastly, there's the issue that if I'm not interested in a topic, it's virtually impossible for me to retain the knowledge. Give me an Asperger's "special interest" and I can give you more facts in an hour than you would want in a lifetime, but if I have no interest, I have no retention. People understandably mistake this for laziness, but it's just the way my mind works.

Black Culture

You could trace the origins of my next special interest back to my friendships with Josh, and later Nick. What followed next was my increasing interest in hip-hop and R&B music, and then I started getting into wearing urban clothing. These are all typical things teenage guys might be interested in, but being autistic, I took it a step further. Obviously, all these things are superficial aspects of African-American culture, but I started wondering why it was that so many American teenagers are drawn to them.

As a kid who had struggled with social skills his whole life, I started observing black culture through the music, through the videos, on TV, etc. I began realizing that black people in many ways seemed to have better social skills than anybody. This sounds like a controversial opinion, but I still stand by it. I started revering African-American culture so much that it wasn't enough for me just to listen to the music, I changed up my whole wardrobe. I started dressing as if I were a black guy as I began to realize that if I just looked to how African-American men handled social inter-actions, I was better off than trying to get feedback, advice, and influences from other Caucasians.

Part of it was me challenging society's assertion that "skin color" doesn't matter. If that were true, there was no reason why I couldn't dress like a black guy. I loved the clothes, and I loved how they looked on me. I finally felt like I had found an identity. Anytime I was talking to a girl I started thinking, "What would a black guy say?" My entire life had been spent getting absolutely zero helpful advice from other people regarding social skills. For some reason with black people, it just wasn't the same. Look, there are plenty of things white people are good at, but for whatever reason, they do not tend to be very good at articulating the social skills that just come naturally to them. Black people, in my experience, are more observant of social interactions, in a very street smart kind of way. Mix that with their natural confidence and sense of style, and they tend to give much more easy and digestible advice, such as "You gotta play it like this" or "If you do this, they're gonna think that." Sorry, but it's true! #CelebrateOurDifferences

Growing up in Maine where black culture is nonexistent, seeing it on TV and in music videos, it seemed so far away and so glamorous. I'm not the only one who felt this way. Let me tell you, as teenagers growing up in an all-white environment like Maine, we *needed* black culture! Everything is just so awkward without it! And so in high school, it's kind of the go-to default for fitting in. And this has been going on since Elvis Presley, it's no secret: white teenagers look to black culture for style and mimic the trends. Almost every single slang expression used in popular culture originates from the African-American community. Knowing the current slang terms (Get lit, Turn up, etc.) and the latest rap songs is crucial to fitting in in high school. So my obsession with black culture wasn't just a random special interest like vacuum cleaners or birds, it actually served a very practical purpose when I was eighteen and nineteen years old. I may not currently be obsessed with black culture like I was during this time, but when I look back at it, I'm not like, "Oh I can't believe I dressed like that." I'm more like, "Yep that makes sense." Being an individual on the spectrum, if it weren't for black culture, I have no idea what I would have done.

When I moved to Florida after graduating high school and all of a sudden black culture was everywhere, I was like a kid in Disney World. Anyone who has lived in the South knows that, in many ways, it's as if segregation never ended. There are white neighborhoods and black neighborhoods so clearly defined that there should be a sign, "Welcome to the black part of town!" And when you leave a sign that says, "Thanks for visiting, please come again!" Living in Broward County where I could see African Americans every day, shop at urban clothing stores, and turn on the radio and hear urban radio stations, it was like gasoline poured on my interest. Almost immediately, it turned to full-on obsession.

I had been obsessed with urban music when I was living in Maine, but I couldn't really connect with black culture at large, because there wasn't any of it around. Living in Florida, my interest basically expanded from black music (Plies, Trina, Keyshia Cole) to all of black culture. At the peak of this phase in 2011, I remember my interest in it being so all-consuming that honestly I don't think I have ever been as interested in anything. It was all I could think about and all I could talk about. I was like a sponge trying to soak up everything there was to know about black culture in the south. Every chance I got, I went to the blackest parts of south Florida and just hung out. I loved it!

The original caption for this was: "So much PBS (that's Pretty Boy Swag)"

I know you're thinking: how did I go into these neighborhoods without causing any problems for myself? In my experience anyone who makes comments like this has never spent any time in these neighborhoods themselves. It's like anywhere else, if you act like you belong there, then you're good. Any friends who ever saw me around black people were amazed at my "black people game." The key was that I didn't have to pretend. I was genuinely immersed in the culture. I listened to the music, I knew all the hottest new "joints," and not even just rap, but R&B too, (which is really much more of a black thing than rap). Not to mention, my closet by this time looked like the urban section of a Burlington Coat Factory. I had all the brands: COOGI, Parish, Akademiks, even Eight 732. I didn't just show up in those neighborhoods wearing Abercrombie & Fitch, I went G'd up from the feet up. This was, at the time, me truly being myself.

Some white people seemed to have the idea that African-Americans react to Caucasians taking an interest in their culture by taking deep offense. Again, I found that these were the people who had never spent any time around African-Americans. To those people I would just ask: if you met a black individual who enjoyed going camping, drinking craft beer, and shopping with you at Whole Foods, would you take offense? Or would you appreciate that you had something in common?

I found that black people recognized the authenticity of my interest, and on top of that, found it hilarious. And that made me feel *really cool*, and rightfully so. In the middle of neighborhoods, stores, and shopping centers that most people I grew up with would be scared to drive through, let alone go out of their way to hang out in, I felt as close to catching the rabbit as I have ever been. When I was in these neighborhoods, I actually felt like I was normal, and like I was a part of something. And for that something to be, of all things, *Southern black culture?!* Do you have any idea how good that felt after almost two decades of feeling like a complete outcast? Unless you have a social skills disability, the answer is no, you have no idea how good it felt.

The Art of Stealing

When college didn't work out, the whole reason I went to Florida had a wrench thrown in it. My mom always said, "Free time is the enemy of Dylan."

I didn't have any money, and my parents didn't want me smoking cigarettes anymore. However, there was no way I was ready to stop smoking yet; it had almost become a miniature special interest for me of trying all the different brands of cigarettes on the market. I decided to get creative. At the time I just had a bike, and I lived a few miles from the mall, so off I went to do what I referred to as "cig hustling." I'd go outside every restaurant and use my line, "Could I give you 50 cents for a cig?" Most people are basic—they just go up and say, "Can I bum a cigarette off you?" That might work sometimes but it was *much* more effective to offer some amount of money, because 9 out of 10 people would be so appreciative of the offer, that they would say, "You can just have one!"—to which I would say, "Thanks! I didn't have 50 cents anyway." 😀 I would bring two empty packs with me, and by the time I left the mall, I would have two full packs of cigarettes.

When I got home I would marvel at all the different kinds of smokes I had gotten, laying them all out on the table like a cigarette buffet. It wasn't structured time, and my parents would not have been happy about how I was spending my days, but it kept me busy and out of trouble.

At this time, I was very much into my clothes and my self-image in general. I had come to create a look for myself that my sister Mariah coined as "Gangsta Prep." My self-esteem was really riding at an all-time high back in those days—I even had a customized fitted hat that read "DIELAWN." If I'm being honest, a big part of it was the amount of success I had with girls in my senior year of high school. I don't know what it was that had the planets so aligned, but from the fall of 2009 to the spring of 2010, I did better with girls than any other time of my life. I could sit here and try to tell you otherwise, but it had a profound effect on how I thought of myself. For a man, loving yourself—even to the point of blind confidence—is an indispensable asset. There are many times where I wish I could go back to those 2010 levels I was hitting.

As I mentioned, one of the aspects of black culture that I was most captivated by in Florida was stores that sold urban menswear. Clothing such as all the brands I listed before, literally weren't sold anywhere in Maine. You couldn't find them! There was a Burlington Coat Factory about four miles from my apartment. I was feeling very confident about myself, and BCF had no one guarding the dressing rooms. So, I would wear pants and long-sleeve shirts, (which Floridians actually do), then I would bring a sh*t ton of clothes into the dressing room, rip off the security tags on half the items, and put them on underneath my street clothes. Then I'd walk out and still be holding a big pile of clothes. Sometimes I'd be wearing three or four t-shirts under my shirt and like three pairs of shorts under my jeans. You could have punched me and I wouldn't have felt it. No one was checking what I'd brought into the dressing room.

There was a security guard at the front of the store. When I was about to leave, I would walk to the front of the store and pause, checking to see if people were getting into motion. They can only get you right as you leave. So I would stop right by the door and look at an item near the exit, as if I was checking something out.

For the most part, this worked. The third time I did this I got a little sloppy. I had tried to swap out a white polo shirt I wanted to cop with an old undershirt I had. As I was heading to the exit, I saw a woman get on her walkie-talkie. I went back to the dressing room and changed back to my other clothes. It worked out fine, but it was nerve-racking!

If you have ever successfully shoplifted before, you know that the thrill of when you first walk out of the store is nothing less than exhilarating. Imagine if I had channeled that energy into something productive . . . 😏

Andy

In the late aughts, there was a burgeoning movement called the "Pickup Artist Community." To sum it up short and sweet, it was basically guys sharing advice and experience on how to attract females. When I first starting reading about this stuff—and, because I can't ever keep my mouth shut—telling people about it, I was mostly met with mocking criticism. Barnes & Noble has an entire aisle dedicated to dating tips for women. And it's funny because if you said to most people, "Men are simple. Women are complicated," most people would agree. There were forums on many PUA (pick-up artist) websites, where you could find a wingman in your area to go out and practice game with, so I made a post with my number.

I really needed a friend I could hang with. I had no structure, no money, and no car. What I was really hoping was to find a wingman with a car, because I was very embarrassed about not having one. It wasn't a big deal to other people, but it was a big deal to me—I hated being "that guy." And that's how I met Andy, a twenty-two-year-old wakeboarder who was going to school for air traffic control. One problem I'd been running into trying to find a wingman, is that with any forum for the improvement of social skills, you're going to get your fair share of weirdos. As soon as I met Andy I knew he was legit. He was just what the doctor ordered. He had a car, he was cool, and he had actually gotten into the PUA thing for insight on how to deal with an on-again-off-again, tumultuous relationship with his girlfriend, who was a blonde pro-wakeboarder (literally). I had enough self-awareness by then to know that Andy was pretty cool to be hanging out with me, so I had better not screw this up. It was a tricky balance because I also didn't want to come off try-hard—there's nothing more repellent than agreeing with everything someone says to make them like you. When you do that, you might as well tell them that you aren't cool enough to hang with them.

The first night we hung out, we went to a festival in Deerfield Beach to try out some openers and routines on girls. The first time

I had gotten drunk was on my eighteenth birthday. Having autism and being developmentally a few years behind my age makes me what most would call a "late-bloomer." So, at nineteen, alcohol was still a very new, very exciting novelty to me. Getting some-body to buy the liquor for me, and then hiding it in a Big Gulp from 7-Eleven—the whole process itself was intoxicating. Needless to say, I got *really* drunk at this festival. I was having a blast and acting wild.

I got the number of a just-my-type girl named Farrah, but after one response she stopped texting back. Normally cooler heads might have prevailed, but as I was trashed I thought, "Let's send her texts spelling out her name letter-by-letter, message-by-message . . ." —for like 100 messages worth of texts. Five minutes later we ran back into her, and she ran up and kicked me as hard as she could! She put her phone up in my face, yelling, "I can't even use my phone because of you assh*le!" One thing they said in all this pickup stuff that really resonated with me was that it's better to evoke a negative emotion out of girls than nothing at all. It's better for her to hate you than to be indifferent, because you have a better shot at turning that into a positive emotion, than if she had no emotion about you at all.

A few days later, out of nowhere, I look at my phone and guess who's calling! I tried to wait for as many rings as possible before picking up, I think I made it like one and a half. Farrah asked if I wanted to go to the movies with her that night! She was going out with a big group of kids, and everyone had dates except her, so she was calling me! 🐶 See? If she hadn't kicked me, she might not have called me. Going to the movies with her and seeing her whole group of friends was one of the first eye-openers for me about the caliber of people in South Florida compared to Maine. There was no better way to say it, they were just cooler. And by that I mean faster-paced, more attractive, and just generally of higher social value. It was pretty awesome getting to meet all these people as Farrah's date. I felt VIP as f*ck. Not only was Farrah just my type (tall and thin), she actually had a great personality, which is equally hot to me. I might have been a little too into her though, because alas, we never went out again. When I asked her why, she said I had been a little much in front of her friends.

As always with me, the problem is never not having balls. 2010 Dylan was very high on himself, and I had been going up to Farrah's friends showing off my hat, being like "Yooo I'm DJ Dielawn—what's good?!" It was very much a character I had become; I remember my sister Mariah saying around this time, "His whole life is basically a comedy act." She hit the nail on the head. Ironically, Farrah kind of proved how great her personality was as she was rejecting me, because most girls will not give you honest feedback. I had to appreciate that because I never would have figured it out on my own.

However I'd behaved with Farrah's friends, that liquor had me way more out of control with Andy the night we met her. I wondered if I'd made a bad enough impression to wreck the friendship before it began, but luckily Andy stuck around. Andy was kind of a punk, and he would talk a lot of trash to me, but his actions said otherwise. Besides, I didn't want a friend who told me what I wanted to hear all the time—that's no fun. And Andy was a very fun, very alpha guy who would always decisively make the plans for what we were going to do, and it was a blast going along for the ride.

I had enough social savvy back then that I felt it was important that I validated Andy's choice to befriend me. When you introduce two friends to each other, you end up looking cool in both of their eyes. If the two of them become friends, it's like your friendship gets solidified in the mix, as the guy who brought them together. I had a feeling Andy was thinking he was my only friend, and I wanted to put a stop to that. I had met another guy named Pete. He was an Asian guy, very smart, also very into pickup, and I knew Andy would think Pete was cool. Watching the two of them meet was epic because the difference between Andy suspecting he was my only friend—versus Andy seeing that not only do I have a social life, but I can bring friends into his world? That was a *big* leap.

Pete was in real estate, and the three of us would hang out weekends at a vacant property he had in Miami. I didn't like South Beach because it was too Latin and Guido, but hanging out with two guys that were older than me in a high-rise apartment in South Beach was an adventure. I'm sure the fact that I never had an older brother, or even an older cousin, had a lot to do with why I liked having male friends that were a few years older.

Telemarketing, Winter 2011

I needed a job and something to do. I was tired of having no money. South Florida is the telemarketing capital of the world, and telemarketing is a very sketchy business. I thought I would be good at it because my voice sounds good on the phone, and I'm not at all shy. But it's hard to sell over the phone—I don't know how anyone does it. The good thing was that I didn't have to make a living at it. I just needed some money that wasn't from my parents, who had me on a limited budget.

I didn't realize how rough telemarketing jobs were. I first took a boiler-room, telemarketing gig offering a deal to go to Disney World. The catch was that you had to sit through a conference where they tried to sell you timeshares. They gave me a script, which to me was like acting. I was very enthusiastic about it and went a little over the top. I would say things like, "You are going to make memories for the rest of your life!" It was fun until I realized I wasn't making any money. I got one deal in two weeks and the woman ended up not paying. It was cool, though, because I got to work with black people. One time the manager yelled at everyone because we weren't upselling enough, then told us to all go home. A sassy old black lady I worked with was like, "Ain't got to tell me twice . . . " It wasn't long before I quit that job for another telemarketing job.

In my new job, I was selling advertisements in a golf magazine that was sent to country clubs. We would call businesses seeing if they wanted to put an ad in the magazine. I really liked this job. There were a lot of people in their twenties and thirties working there. One guy lived in Deerfield Beach, so we agreed to carpool every day. It was a hustle every day to make sales. It was one of those offices with no cubicles, so everybody could hear what everybody else was saying. I loved it at times because occasionally I'd be on a funny phone call and it was like I was on stage.

Once again, I was the comedian at work. I thought that I had matured beyond being the workplace comedian at this point in my life, as that behavior had gotten me fired from the pizza place three years earlier, but I hadn't. With the open floor plan of the office it really lent itself to being my own personal stage. It turned into more and more of me playing up my persona at work, trying to make people laugh. And don't get it twisted, they were laughing, and would often feed into it and egg me on because I was so entertaining. I would banter about all the usual stuff—about my dating experiences: "I hung out with this girl last weekend . . ." and African-American culture: "I think I'm gonna go eat lunch in the black area today, anybody got any recommendations?" My boss happened to be black. He would pick on me, but in a funny way. I was just this over-the-top character of Dielawn, the white kid from Maine who was obsessed with black people. I would say it was an exaggerated version of myself, but that was literally who I was at the time.

I loved this job and I couldn't wait to wake up at 6 a.m. to go to work every day. However, my sales were not great; I couldn't close a deal. I don't really know how to talk someone into doing something without being pushy. I realized that presentation skills are not what you need to succeed in sales—what you need are *persuasion* skills. I'm great at presentation, and I'm great at persistence, but I'm not great at persuasion. They fired me after . . . (guess how long) one month on the job.

As soon as I got called into the room, I knew I was done. Like I had heard many times before, they said that they liked me, but it just wasn't working out. They said it wasn't my work ethic because they tracked how many phone calls we made and I was among the top five "dialers" in the office. But they pointed out that

that made it even worse. With all the effort I was putting in, my numbers were still dismal. Additionally, my presence in the office was constantly "taking people off the phone." So, basically I was too entertaining for my co-workers to focus on selling. I know if my sales had been better, they probably wouldn't have been firing me. But since they were, I think they wanted to help me out with some parting advice: they really emphasized that I was being inappropriate in the workplace.

Everything about this firing felt all too familiar. Once again, my lack of social skills and having very little filter had done me in at a job. 😖

My Grandparents in Florida, 2011

When I was living in Florida, my paternal grandparents, Nana and Papa, were about an hour away in West Palm Beach. They would often drive down on Saturdays to take me out for lunch, buy me some things I needed, and do something I enjoyed. My seventy-plus-year-old Jewish grandparents, especially my grandfather, were having a hard time relating to me because of my new black persona, but they still went out of their way to try. I look back and really appreciate how much effort they made to connect with me. Most grandparents would have given up and either ignored me or waited until I moved on to a new special interest. But week after week, they came down to see me.

I didn't have my car when I first arrived, so when they visited, I wanted to go through Riviera Beach, an almost all-black city in Palm Beach County. They said, "We don't want to drive through Riviera Beach, but we will take you through the rough part of West Palm Beach."

I didn't even know that there was a black area in West Palm Beach. I said, "But I won't see things like a group of black people sitting outside listening to music." Papa very confidently said, "Oh yeah, you will." We went, and it was every bit as awesome as I hoped it would be.

As I've mentioned, I've always loved cats. Nana found a place in South Florida where there are close to a hundred cats in a relatively small space. It's a cat shelter with many, many, many cats! She took me there a couple of times so that I could just spend an hour petting all the cats. She didn't enjoy spending more than ten minutes in there, so she would patiently wait in the car until I was done. That was very exciting for me and very nice of her.

I had started smoking cigarettes in high school. Papa was an ex-smoker and he hated that I had taken up the habit. He offered me a deal to get me to stop smoking. He said, "I'll agree to pay you an undisclosed amount of money every month for five years if you'll agree to stop smoking." My parents loved the plan except for one glitch—it didn't start until the end of the year. Papa's logic was that I needed some time to get the whole idea of smoking out of my system. He said, "Until the end of the year, you can smoke as much as you want. You can smoke Pall Malls, you can smoke Newports, you can smoke Marlboro Lights, you can smoke Camel Crushes, you can smoke L&Ms, you can smoke Benson and Hedges, you can smoke Parliaments, you can smoke Kools . . ." After that, the offer is on the table. But if you start smoking again, I'll take my money back at the same rate I put it in for every month you smoke."

I went home and very proudly started lighting up in front of my parents. In my mind it was okay with my parents that I smoked because my grandfather had said it was. I didn't think they would have a different opinion. They yelled, "What the hell are you doing?" and I said, "But Papa said I could smoke as much as I wanted to until January first! He said I could smoke Winstons, I could smoke Lucky Strikes, I could smoke Basics, I could smoke Marlboro blend 27's, I could smoke Marlboro blend 54's, I could smoke clove cigarettes, I could smoke Camel Turkish golds, I could smoke Camel Turkish silvers, I could smoke Camel Turkish royals . . ." I assumed that my parents had signed off on this plan, but they were outraged. They didn't want me smoking so much, and they definitely didn't want me smoking right in front of the house or by the windows because it made the house smell like a dive bar.

I liked smoking. It was fun! And there's the concept of a "cig convo." Anyone who's ever smoked knows exactly what I am talking about. A "cig convo" is a conversation you strike up with a stranger as you're both blazing. These casual conversations helped me immediately fit in with anyone else who smoked. They eliminated the awkward moments of small talk that I struggle with when meeting someone new. We could just talk about the different brands of cigs. In under a minute, I could connect with another smoker in a way that I could not possibly do in most situations. Eventually, I did stop smoking tobacco. I'm sure that I never would have quit if my grandfather hadn't put that deal in front of my face.

My grandparents did eventually cave to my constant requests and took me to eat at a rib place in Riviera Beach. We were the only Caucasoid peoples to come in or out during the entire meal. That was very exciting for me—not so much for my grandparents, but they did it anyway.

Grandparents often have a hard time connecting with their autistic grandkids. They don't know much about autism because it was never spoken of in their day. What usually happens is they either blow that grandkid off completely or spend all their time telling the parents what they're doing wrong. They'll say things like, "He just needs some discipline," or, "That kid needs a good kick in the ass." This just alienates them even more from their grandkid and usually from the kid's parents as well. Grandparents like that usually stop visiting and stop getting invited to anything involving the autistic grandkid. The kid doesn't like them around and neither do the parents, so why bother having them there, causing stress for everyone?

If you think about it, your role as a grandparent is pretty easy: love your grandkids. You don't have to discipline them, you're not responsible for "raising them right," you don't have to make them do their homework or eat their vegetables. Just love them as they are, that's all. But some grandparents can't even do that simple task, so they end up having no relationship with their autistic grandchild. In that case, everyone loses.

Swag Pays the Bills

People say "swag" doesn't pay the bills—I bet none of them grew up struggling to interact with other people. Theodore Roosevelt said, "The most important single ingredient in the formula of success is knowing how to get along with people"—and that's a pretty undisputed fact. Well what is "swag"? It's the impression you make on other people. You can laugh at me for using the word, but are you disputing that it's a concept? I wasn't born with any of it. I've tried to learn it over the years, and I'm probably still working on it. But I can tell you that it absolutely does matter. Show me someone who talks about swag as some foolish thing that shouldn't be strived for, and I'll show you someone who never had to work for it and appreciate it—or who just doesn't have it at all.

It could be said that people with swag have an ability to effortlessly present as "cool." Well, what is "Being Cool?" At it's very essence, being cool is showing social intelligence. Yet, we scoff at the notion of "being cool" like it's silly and meaningless. There is nothing silly and meaningless about social intelligence. Cool gets you more dates, cool gets you more friends, and more friends gets you more connections. For God's sake, cool won Obama a presidency! So yes, swag *does* in fact pay the bills.

Going to Jail for the First Time: Shoplifting, Winter 2011

In South Florida, every mall has its own personality. The Boca Town Center was the ritzy mall, Coral Square was the suburban mall, Sawgrass was the mall you got lost in, and then there was the Broward Mall. Pete had told me never to go there because it was "ghetto," so naturally I was dying to check it out. I decided to be productive one day and kill two birds with one stone—I would go visit the Broward mall *and* get some shoplifting in. I'm not going to say I liked riding the bus because I didn't have my car, but I will say taking public transportation sure brought an extra level of authenticity to the whole hood experience. The Broward Mall was in Plantation off of Broward Boulevard, and I could barely keep from beaming ear-to-ear as I checked out the area. Every car in sight had rims! There was a Church's Chicken, MetroPCS, and of course, the staple of every hood, the "Discount Beauty Supply." This wasn't the rundown, depressing hood—this was the flashy hood, like something out of a Gucci Mane video.

I stepped into the mall on my mission to get some new clothes. It's hard to believe I used to dedicate entire days to this venture. You have to remember—when I was nineteen, my maturity level was like that of a fourteen or fifteen-year-old, and if you look at it through that lens it's actually not so shocking at all. You could tell this was an urban mall because the Macy's was carrying COOGI shirts. I took three of them into the dressing room, tugged at the security tags until they broke off, threw the shirts in my backpack and headed toward the exit. I did my trick of chilling by the door to see if anyone was moving into action, and the coast was clear. Next I went to Dillard's. I had heard that Dillard's had next-to-no security, and I heard right. I walked out of there with some Sean John shorts and a Rocawear polo. 💯

The rush of getting away with it had me flying high. This was about more than getting some free clothes—this was about pulling off something that, although it's not positive, does require a certain savvy, a certain craftiness. Forget reading social cues—you have to be able to read a million different variables and get inside everyone else's head in the store if you want to get away with shoplifting! Suffice it to say, this was NOT the kind of thing I should be good at. Probably a lot of neurotypical people wouldn't be good at it! However, what a lot of neurotypical people probably *would* have been good at, is getting out of Macy's and Dillard's and quitting while they were ahead. It was like when I was at a P.E.T. meeting with my parents and teachers in seventh grade and they asked me why I was, as they said, "pushing limits." I said, "Because I'm always feeling around for the walls, until I bang up against one, and then I know that's as far as I can push it." The problem was even once I found the walls, I liked to stay right at them or try and see if I could expand them over time.

So on I went to Sears. I was getting cocky because I had just gotten away with stealing from two stores—why would Sears be any different? They had some fresh U.S. Polo Association shirts on sale. Some people would clown me for preferring the cheap knock-off Polo instead of the authentic Ralph Lauren Polo. My logic was that U.S.P.A., despite being an imitation brand, was actually *more* hood, because in the hood you will see more people wearing U.S.P.A. than the real thing. Where was the lie?

Back in high school, Nick's sister Teena once told me that gray was my color, and I never forgot her advice. I saw a gray U.S.P.A. shirt with the big pony logo in dark blue, on sale for $34.99. I actually had enough money to buy it, but that wasn't what I came for. I took my backpack and dropped it in the lawn-mower section, went back, got the shirt, and then threw it in my backpack. I didn't even do my trick of chilling by the door to see if anyone was getting into motion before walking out. And to top it all off, I was getting so sloppy I didn't even walk outside, I actually walked BACK into the mall! Suddenly I heard, "Excuse me sir! I need the merchandise!"

As you can imagine, my heart sank. But there is a protective reflex in my brain that works kind of like a trampoline—as soon as things go bad, my mind immediately thinks, "Everything's fine, this is no big deal!" I kept telling myself I would be fine, and I'd talk my way out of it. The security guard walked me back to a private room that they apparently had just for this purpose. I was going to cooperate, so of course I handed over the merchandise. I got a look at the security room and realized that there was a huge disparity in store security. Dillard's and Macy's were both so easy! I assumed Sears would be the same—but no, Sears had 1984 levels of surveillance. "I knew he was gon' do it! He was lookin' around way too much!" a female security guard exclaimed. The place looked like a high-tech police station with giant monitors up and down the walls, it was clear they had been watching me the whole time.

My protective reflexes telling me "Everything will be okay!" would have been accurate, except that I didn't have my ID on me at the time. Normally for shoplifting you would just get a ticket, but because they couldn't verify who I was, they were forced to take me to jail. I was relieved that the police officer who showed up was friendly. He asked me why I did it, and then told me it was a bummer I had to go to jail over a thirty dollar shirt. He then got on the phone with another officer, who asked if I was being cooperative and he said, "Yes, he is very cooperative." Even though I was in handcuffs, that was a nice compliment to hear.

The security woman started looking throw my backpack at the other clothes in there, "COOGI???" She said, obviously surprised (and maybe a little impressed) by my urban taste in menswear. She saw where the security tags had been ripped off, and she knew what was up. But you only get busted from the store that catches you—"Those ain't from my store, I ain't gon' worry about that," she said. So I ended up going to jail with all the other stolen clothes I had gotten away with. Even though I got caught for one shirt, it was like a net profit.

I had previously had a *lot* of encounters with the police, so I wasn't all that surprised that I finally found myself in jail. I felt like it was a rite of passage, the type of thing everybody had to do once!

Not only did the Fort Lauderdale jail have lots of black guys, they weren't just any black guys. They had gold teeth, dreads, and face tattoos. It was a pretty safe bet to assume these guys were the real deal—after all, we were literally in jail. I remembered all the times one of my peers had quipped, "You would get shot if you ever went to the hood," thinking they were being original. I thought, here's my chance—let's win them over.

I started asking the guys in there what type of rap music they liked. I asked them if they liked Plies, who was my favorite rapper at the time. MUSIC INFO: There are certain hip-hop artists that are more popular with white audiences and certain artists more popular with black audiences. Plies fit into the latter category, so the great thing was, nobody expected a white guy to be asking about Plies, let alone know his entire discography. Plies also happens to be from Florida, so he's really huge there and I knew they would all know him. That was something we bonded over. Plies had a new single out, "Really From Da Hood," where he says, "I'm from da hood though, like da hood though, like really, really, really from da hood though." Because of his thick southern accent, I thought the lyrics were "I'm from da hood dawg, like da hood dawg." I started singing it like that, and they thought it was absolutely hilarious. It felt really great to genuinely be interested in a culture I could share with other people. They also gave me some advice: they asked me what I was there for, and then one guy told me, "Bruh, look around, nobody else is here for shoplifting, that's just some dumb sh*t." Because this was coming from people that seemed to accept me and people I thought were cool, I actually paid attention.

There's one image that has stayed burned in my mind. If you've ever been to jail, you know that the set-up is reminiscent of a school cafeteria with the round tables and attached stools. I remember sitting there while four or five black guys stood around me, and you would've thought it was a comedy show, the way I had them laughing. I was asking them about the "hoodest" parts of Florida so I could hit them up when I got out. They told me that in Southern Florida, the farther south you go (like towards Miami), the harder it gets. They found my desire to be black hysterical, and not offensive in the least. I remember thinking, if only every person who ever repeated that garbage of "You'd get shot if you ever went to the hood" . . . if ONLY they could see me now.

But jail wasn't all fun, if you can believe that. The downside to jail was that it's the kind of place that doesn't have to give you answers that make any sense. They don't have to explain anything to you. For someone with autism, that is horrible. Even if I don't like what's happening, I always need to know why. As a matter of fact, *especially* if I don't like what's happening. I usually knew what was happening to me but I could rarely figure out why. For most people with autism, the "why" is more important than the "what." I didn't like not knowing how long I was going to be in there. The legal system is arcane—I didn't understand how things worked, and I bet half the people working there didn't know how it worked. So while I was having fun hanging with the guys in there, I was still anxious to know when I would be able to leave. Finally, I got an answer. One of the guards told me I would probably be out by the end of the day. But then someone said, "You can't believe what the guards tell you. Just because he said that doesn't mean anything."

I said, "Who can I believe? Where can I get a f*cking answer?" I wasn't okay with vague answers and not getting any information. I was being so annoying by asking so many questions that the guards probably went to one of their bosses and said, "Hey, we have to get this guy out of here. He's driving us nuts!" I really think that might have happened. Because it was clear that I wasn't playing dumb—I was being genuinely naïve and annoying.

The staff informed me I would be able to bond out by the end of the day. One of my cellmates told me, "Man, just relax, you're not going to be in here for long, so just go to sleep and know that you only have a few hours left."

I thought about that and started to feel pretty lucky because I wasn't going to be there for a long time, unlike a lot of the guys there. I relaxed and fell asleep. Several hours later, one of the guards knocked on my door and told me I could bond out.

I got to the bond office and everyone was just sitting around. There was a desk with some sassy diverse ladies, not at all unlike the DMV. My bond was twenty-five dollars. At the time my parents had given me a Visa Bucks card. The card was made for teenagers, so parents could load money on it electronically but limit the use of it. I thought I had enough money on it to get out, but Visa Bucks charges processing fees. Also, the system charged inmates a small daily fee for being in jail. I don't understand how that's legal. "We're going to bring you to jail and then we're going to charge you," seems very third-world to me. I know you committed a crime, but you're supposed to be innocent until proven guilty. No matter how many times you explain it to me, forcing someone to pay to be held against their will still seems very un-American.

When they called me up to bail out and then said my card only paid for twenty dollars of my twenty-five-dollar bail, I asked frantically if I could call someone to get more money and figure something out. The clerk who was dealing with me yelled, "He's a no-go. Next!" That could have easily been one of the worst moments of my life—all that buildup to finally get released from jail, and then getting turned away in a matter of seconds for something totally out of my control? 😨 It really would have been the ultimate "change-of-plans" situation that people on the spectrum loathe so greatly. But before I could completely panic, a guy from my cell block who was sitting nearby overheard me and said, "What? Is he five dollars short?" He had five dollars in cash, and the guard asked the clerk if that was allowed. There was a pause where everyone was kind of shocked, and the clerk said in a very surprised tone, "If he wants to give it to him, he can."

Much like the guy who hauled my mom's Yukon XL out of the snow, this guy stepped in at the absolute eleventh hour to save my ass. You can't write this stuff, and it wraps up my whole experience in jail with the perfect ending: not only did I make some friends, one of them cared enough to help me get the hell out of there! As the receptionist took the five dollars, she told me, "It's very rare that this happens." She didn't have to tell me, though—I was beside myself with appreciation, and I had the perfect way to thank him. As the guards handed me back my bag filled with clothes I had shoplifted from other stores, I asked him if he needed anything. He ended up taking the shirt I had worn to the mall which was a black long-sleeved American Eagle shirt. He was all, "Bruh, that's perfect, good looks!!" It was great to repay this good Samaritan and be able to give him something back. I felt like the world's most virtuous shoplifter.

That was that: I was out of jail.

I hadn't told my parents about this adventure yet. And then I realized that I didn't have to tell them at all. There is a certain affinity that you develop for things when they are one hundred percent yours. Living in Florida with my parents thousands of miles away, gave me the first experiences of my life that felt like they were completely mine. No doubt they would, and did, find out eventually but in that moment, walking out of jail was a feeling I wanted to keep all to myself. I caught the bus and headed home.

I had been worried about my cat, Beautiful Boy. There was a girl named Emily in the program. She was kind of cute, and we had hung out together a few times. I have no idea why the program accepted her, because she was totally neurotypical and didn't seem to have any problems. It felt pretty cool to be the guy that became friends with her because I felt like she saw me as the closest to normal out of the bunch. I turned my phone back on and, thank God, there were a bunch of texts from her wondering where I was, saying that she was taking care of my cat.

So, that was my first experience in jail. I have to say it was kind of fun. I went through it all by myself, and no one even knew it happened. I hold it as a cool memory for that reason, but I would later learn that jail is definitely only cool the first time.

The Best Month Ever, April 2011

By March of that year, after eleven long months, my parents decided I had suffered enough relying on public transportation and returned my car to me. You know how sometimes in life you build things up so much in your head, but when they finally come to pass they aren't what you had envisioned? Getting my car back wasn't like that at all. This was one of those *very* rare occasions where things played out just as fantastically as what I had pictured in my head.

I had been trying relentlessly to land a job in a mall. I have always loved the mall—just walking in and getting hit with that mall smell puts me in a good mood. But after three jobs that didn't pan out, I stopped trying. If I couldn't have a mall job, my second choice was a job where I could be around . . . guess who! You already know.

I always loved Boston Market. When I was a kid, the closest Boston Market was in Massachusetts. My dad would take me to Celtics games, and even though I didn't care for basketball, I liked spending time with him. He liked Boston Market, too, so on the way home we would stop there. We always said, "Why can't they put one of these in Maine?" It was cheap, fast, and relatively healthy. It was the treat of the year for me. Now I lived right across the street from a Boston Market. Driving by one day, I looked in and saw all black faces. I walked right in. They were hiring, and I got the job.

My first night working there, our boss let us take home a plate of the food getting thrown out, as much we wanted. Right before-hand he gave us a very stern warning, "I swear to GOD if ANY OF YOU say a g*ddamn word about this, I will tell them on my life it was you and who are they gonna believe!? You will be F*CKED do you understand me?!" I realized he was probably going through this spiel because of me, so I let them all know "I ain't snitchin." That made them all laugh, and I would never in a million years rat somebody out for being generous and bending the rules like that; it makes me sad that he even had to say that.

My car at the time was an Oldsmobile Eighty-Eight, (very confusing name, it was actually a '96). If you Google this car you'll see why I referred to it as my "gangsta whip." It had just been the random used car my parents decided to get me, but God must have had a hand in their decision because it fit my image to a T. You know how those big, long cars are either old person cars, or black person cars? It was one of those big ole' granddaddy Oldsmobiles and I loved it. Andy was still friends with me, and it was great once again validating his choice to befriend me by having him see me finally get my car. He would mercilessly tease me about my "gangsta whip" being a grandma car. I think he knew deep down that it was a straight-up black person's car but didn't want to admit it.

I thought that getting a car in Florida would do the same thing to my social life that it had in Maine three years earlier. I thought things would just explode, and that having a car would lead to meeting many new people. I came to find out it was different in Florida. It didn't seem to command the same effect that getting a car had in Maine.

Despite my interest at the time, there was still a part of me that wasn't done making up for lost time growing up. I was very much stuck in high school mode; I was a high schooler in every way except the school part. I still really wanted acceptance by other white kids just to prove to myself I could do it. Most white people in South Florida are middle to upper class. It seemed that all the kids I wanted to hang out with had a car themselves or knew someone with a car. I started wishing they would just use me for my car! Even if one kid is using you, it leads to other opportunities. Meeting that kid's friends and then meeting their friends' friends, that's how you develop a social circle. So that had me disappointed. I tried looking at it as "finding out who my real friends were," but it didn't make me feel better.

Dating

Outside of a romantic situation, I generally hate touching people. I hate hugging people. I hate shaking hands. Even with a good friend or family member, I wish we would just never, ever touch. Like, if it's a guy friend, we don't *ever* need to touch, bro. Don't get me wrong, I do it anyway, at the times when I am supposed to . . . I just don't like it.

My experience with girls is oddly super-similar to my job experience. I'm really good at getting jobs but not at keeping them. I am also really good at getting girls . . . . but not so good at keeping them. Was I always good at this? No, and I wasn't always good at getting jobs either, but over time I got pretty good at it.

The girl situation is like the job situation, except of course it's more extreme. A girl has not put you through HR training and orientation. She hasn't given you all the paperwork to get you started as a "member of the team." Oh no, if you mess up, a girl is going to move right on to the next five guys who are direct-messaging her, with no hesitation. When I was in Utah, my counselor (probably the only counselor who's ever helped me at all) said, "You know, Dylan, it could be a lot worse."

I thought about that, and now I have a good perspective on it. Girls treat me like I am a boy band. What I mean by that is they treat me like I'm the Backstreet Boys: they like me a lot for a little while, and then as soon as 'NSYNC comes along, it's "Bye Bye Bye." (Sorry, I couldn't resist.) Next thing I know they are tearing all my posters off their bedroom walls and moving on to the next big thing! And I never end up being the Justin Timberlake of that boy band. No, no, I always end up being the Chris Kirkpatrick or the Kevin Richardson of the band. Who the hell are those guys? Exactly! But my counselor was right: it could be a lot worse than girls treating me like a boy band. At least I got my poster on that bedroom wall! I got my fifteen minutes of fame, my moment in the sun.

Jail for the Second Time!

In Florida, they have nightclubs devoted to teens and people who are under twenty-one. There were two of them near me, Club Cinema and Club Boca. I'm always up for a social challenge and there is no challenge like going to a crowded nightclub. Clubs are super-overheated, with *no* personal space. They are dark, loud, and—if you're a male—people will most likely be hostile toward you. Not to mention, if you want water *(and you do)*, it's eight dollars! You couldn't create in a lab a more miserable environment for someone with autism. But when you're chasing the rabbit, that's no excuse! So I went anyway. Sometimes I just decide I am going to live my life as if I don't have autism, and this was one of those times.

I went to Club Boca with Daniel, a friend I had made. Daniel was a good wingman—he had game, he was six feet tall, and girls thought he was good-looking, but not so good looking that he completely overshadowed me (like Nick back in high school). He wasn't judgmental and he was very laid back—just the type of neurotypical person that makes a good friend for me.

As much as I was up for a challenge, these clubs are NO place to be sober. In Florida, when you're underage and want to get alcohol, the black parts of town are incredibly useful. Before we went to the club, Daniel and I went to my go-to spot, 101 Liquors, less than a half a mile away from my apartment. This place was exciting as hell to me every time I went in. As soon as you walked in, you saw life-sized cardboard cutouts of different hip-hop artists advertising alcoholic beverages—you had Diddy with his Cîroc, Trina next to some Nuvo, and they'd actually have rap music playing over the store speakers! Now, I just have to reiterate, having lived in a culturally homogenous state like Maine for eighteen years, little things like this were just so thrilling to experience for me. When I would go to 101 Liquors, one of two things would happen: if the right manager was working, this guy would just be like, "You're twenty-one, right?"—which was hilarious, because I didn't even look *my* age at the time (which was nineteen). Or if someone else was working and they ID'd me, I'd simply go back outside, post up against the wall, and ask a random black person going in if they could help me out. They'd be like, "Aiight, whatchu want?" and I'd give them the money. They'd go in and get it for me, come back out, and I'd give them a tip. It was so chill, why can't all of life be like a black liquor store?

That night with Daniel, I got a giant bottle of McCormick's with some Mountain Dew, and we brought it back to the club to drink outside before we went in. We were there about an hour before the club opened, and there were a bunch of other kids hanging out in the parking lot. I can't overstate the high caliber of people that you see in South Florida—it's almost . . . inspirational. I saw a bunch of girls I'd want to get with and guys I'd want to be friends with. I had bought cups at the liquor store, too, and I started offering everybody shots. I didn't expect this stunt to work as well as it did. Kids were swarming around me like, "Dude, you're the man!" and "Omg, thank you!" It was back to that same idea of giving something out to attract people to me. I looked at it like a "friendship loss-leader." And hey, there was *plenty* of vodka to go around. This is where my memory of the night starts to get hazy, but I remember drunkenly walking around the parking lot, passing the vodka to everybody, having a great time.

By the time we went in, I was so completely hammered that I actually blacked out on the dance floor. I remember Daniel and a few of the kids I had met outside telling me to get up, and then several of them attempting to lift me up, but I had kept drinking to the point where I didn't know what was going on. I was literally passed out in the middle of the club—I mean, come on—I was just begging to get arrested. Surprise! That's exactly what happened.

When they processed me at the jail, I was still laughing and having a good time. They threw me in a holding cell, where they put four or five people, and for some reason there was a working phone in there with us. I stayed drunk the whole night, not a bad way to serve your time. Unlike the last experience, they gave me an exact answer for when I would be leaving: "You'll be gone by the morning." they told me. The next morning, as soon as I sobered up, I was walking out.

Palm Beach County Jail was not very scary. It was mostly old white guys. When I walked out of jail, I found myself in the middle of nowhere. Outside was literally just an open field of grass with nothing around. Luckily, Daniel knew how to drive, so he took care of my car after I got arrested. I called him, and he picked me up. I ended up having to do two weeks of community service at a local antique store, where I just folded clothes the whole time.

It may be hard to believe, but looking back, this was a great point in my life. Despite spending a night in jail, my life has rarely been as good as June of 2011. I look at that mugshot, and I had a fresh haircut, I was thin, I looked muscular, young and tan. It was all a direct reflection of the fact that I had a job, I had an interest I was now surrounded by, I had my car, and I had made some friends. On top of all that, the pop music on the radio at the time was AWESOME. (Britney Spears, "Till the World Ends," anybody?) This time of my life was so exciting and special for me, that it almost feels like it didn't happen. Do you, the reader, have any memories that, as they get further in the rearview, begin to seem like they were a dream? Thank God I have that mugshot, I guess! It serves as a permanent reminder of what I see as a peak time in my life. That tells you something about how my life has gone!

Courtesy of the Palm Beach County Sheriff's Office

Mandy

Even though I had a few wins here and there with the girl thing, the months after I got my car back were just more of the same old, same old with girls. Nothing ever turned into anything more than a hookup, which was never what I really wanted. And then I met Mandy. I'll be the first to tell you that generally speaking, there's no such thing as a girl who's "different" or "not like that"—girls are girls. But if there was ever a female who could put up a good argument against that theory, it was Mandy. I met her the same way I did most girls back then, just a random add on Facebook— except this time, *she added me,* just out of left field. Everything about

Mandy was out of left field. We started talking and for once, every-thing went right. She liked me right out of the gate and didn't play any games about wanting to get to know me.

We talked for about a week and then had our "first date." I picked her up in the Oldsmobile, and we went to see the Justin Timberlake movie, *Friends with Benefits*. Again, everything went right. My Oldsmobile Eighty-Eight had that wonderful bench seat up front, so you could be driving and have a girl cuddling next to you just like you were in the movies. Everything I said was funny, everything I did was cute. It was a first date that could give anything in a Justin Timberlake movie a run for its money. However, this definitely wasn't my first "first date" to be like a real-life rom-com. As excited as I was, I was pretty skeptical that Mandy wouldn't be just another brief fling that fizzled out as fast as it started. To my surprise though, she really wasn't playing games. We kept talking and kept hanging out, and before I knew it, I had myself a girlfriend.

I had always seen being in a relationship as a sort of Holy Grail in life. In high school I used to see people making out by their lockers and couples posting pictures on MySpace where the caption would be the date they got together, you know: "6/14/08 <333." It hurt every single time: from this deep place inside, I felt very strongly, "That should be me." Now, out of deep left field on July 30, 2011, I'd gotten what I wanted.

And as it turned out, Mandy was really the perfect match for me. Her last boyfriend was named Shamar Jackson. She was white like me, but I was the first white guy she had ever dated, which thrilled me to no end, and I still think is pretty badass. I promise I'm not making this up. She had previously lived in a really rough neighborhood, so you can imagine we had plenty to talk about. We would go to the mall and walk around for hours doing cute teenage-couple-y things like testing perfumes and colognes at the counter. Not much different from any other couple, except the mall was the Lauderhill Mall in Fort Lauder-dale, and guess who else went there! We walked around for hours without seeing another white person, which I loved and apparently she was used to!

One of our cutest inside things was arguing over what would be a "ghetto" photo collage on Facebook. In case you're not aware, on social media teenagers often decorate their photos with graphics and words (or at least they did in 2011). Well, people from the hood would tend to decorate their photos a certain way, while people from the suburbs decorated them in a certain way. I would point to a collage a white chick from the suburbs made, (like my sister Lilly who put one up with a bunch of hearts and soccer balls) and I'd say to Mandy, "That collage, that is *HOOD!*" And she would say, "Noooo, oh my God, that's not hood at all!" One day she took a picture of us making out at the Lauderhill Mall, edited it and posted it on my wall. "There!" she said, "That is a ghettoed-out picture of us for real." And she had swagged it out: it was tinted with a sepia tone, and she had "7-30-11" in big letters with hearts all over the place. At the bottom she put "HateOnIt; #$WAGG." After all those times seeing other people post couple collages with their anniversary date, I finally had one of my own. How could it get better than this? 🖤

Mandy and I were even "Facebook official." As you can imagine, all the other girls I knew who hadn't committed to me took notice—big time.

This one chick, Rebecca Markusfeld, who'd been flirting with me forever but would never hang out, started getting really jealous. I could tell because every time she referred to Mandy, she would purposely say her name wrong as "Maddy." 😂 This was what I'd always wanted, and I'd always thought that if I got it, I would be happy and everything would be perfect. And it was for a minute, don't get me wrong—but it wasn't all sunshine and rainbows. The first reality of having a girlfriend I had to face was that just like a job, there's never a guarantee you'll keep it. Except it's like a job that you're not just *financially* attached to—you're *emotionally* attached to it, and there are lots of other guys lining up to try and steal your job.

There was this other guy Mandy had been friends with for a long time who, of course, liked her. This guy was objectively better-looking than me; like if I was an eight, he was at least a nine—he had the six-pack and everything. Apparently they got along really well, and all her friends were telling her to dump me and get with him. Maybe some guys are good at "playing it cool" about this kind of thing, but I am not one of those guys. I would have a hard time acting cool about this if it were just a random girl I wanted to get with, but now this was my official girlfriend! 😵

For a few weeks this sort of competition was going on between me, the boyfriend, and this other dude, Ross, who was running an insurgent campaign for my girlfriend. I knew that they hung out a lot—that was the thing, see—he was in her social circle, whereas I was just this guy none of her friends knew. But Mandy was very trustworthy, (or a very good actress) and obviously I will never know for sure, but I highly doubt she was cheating on me. Still, I was horrified about the idea of losing her, and I had never been in this situation before: my instincts were to get super-mad and super-jealous. (I know—the secret to keeping a girl interested, right?)

The night things finally culminated was right after our two-month anniversary. We hadn't officially broken up, but she had said she wanted us to slow things down a little bit, probably (in hindsight) because she wasn't sure if she wanted to be with Ross. So there I was, hanging out with Andy, on a night when Mandy had gone to a homecoming dance with Ross. She swore up and down that they were going "as friends," and Andy had told me I needed to let her figure out what she wanted because being controlling would just backfire. I was actually okay because the deal was that I had taken her out the night before and he was taking her to homecoming, and then she was supposedly going to finally make a decision between the two of us. I just wanted to stop wondering what was going to happen, and honestly, if the way for me to get an answer was her going to homecoming with him, then it was worth it. Don't get me wrong—I was still a train wreck about it, though. *My girlfriend was spending the night with another guy. How was I supposed to think about anything else?*

Andy knew a lot about females, and he was trying to coach me on how to keep a girlfriend interested. He had an article he was reading to me with all sorts of deep psychological insight, like how you're supposed to emulate their father, spark their emotions, etc. So I was listening to him tell me all this stuff you have to do, and at one point I said, "Can't you just have a relationship and not always have to worry about something happening?"—and he said, "No!" That shut me up.

It was something of an epiphany for me, another moment that opened my eyes. Thank God he stopped me from blowing Mandy's phone up that night because miraculously she called me after her date with Ross. I don't know what Ross did that night, but she told me she didn't feel "that way" about him, and she wanted to be with me! I had won! I can't say I was surprised . . . but I was pretty f*cking surprised. I had beaten out a neurotypical guy who went to school with her, a guy who had lots of females lining up, a guy who even had me beat in the looks department. Like everything with Mandy, this went against everything life had taught me to expect. Remember the look on Donald Trump's face during his acceptance speech? I knew just how he felt. How rude of Ross not to call me and concede like Hillary did!

Things with Mandy survived for a little while longer, but this was toward the end of my time in Florida, and my life was heading off track (again). Who knows what kind of mess that relationship could have devolved into if I hadn't moved—I'm kind of glad I can say that my moving was the reason it ended. ☺ We stayed in touch for a little while after I moved, but eventually she got another boyfriend and cut me off. She ended up dating another white guy! I must have left her wanting more I guess. ☺ I did find her not too long ago on Facebook just to see how she looks now . . . and she got even hotter! It's always great to see an ex who is still good-looking years later, it's like a validation of what you actually had. It works the other way too,

I knew a guy whose ex-girlfriend chopped all her hair off, and got way too many facial piercings, and I could see in his face the disappointment when he saw her again.

Deciding to Leave Florida, Late 2011

Another good title of this book could have been *What Goes Up Must Come Down* because every good period of my life has been followed by a bad one. I have put a lot of effort into forgetting that this ever happened, but I will tell you that in November 2011, I got hopped up on some pills I should not have been prescribed, and I started researching Afro-centrism. I stayed up for several nights listening to podcasts by Tariq Nasheed, (a popular activist). Because of my interest at the time, combined with my mental state, I took the ideas way too far. This included me going full anti-white and saying a lot of mean things about my own family. For me, it is the most cringe-worthy episode of my entire life, and that is a high bar. I know what you're thinking, "Dylan taking something too far? That's crazy!"

It was incredible, because despite being out of my mind and talking like a crazy person, Mandy stayed on the phone with me for hours, night after night, never losing patience with me. That incident lasted about a week, but there were other issues too.

I had kept my job at Boston Market for a record six months, the longest job I had ever kept up to that point. However, I'd been written up twice for being late—one more strike and I was gone. Shockingly enough, when I stayed up for days on end researching Black Supremacy materials, it resulted in me oversleeping and missing a shift. Getting fired from Boston Market brought my life to a halt; like getting thrown off a moving train. Then it got worse: I would leave the sliding glass door in my apartment cracked open for my cat Beautiful Boy to go in and out, and just a few days after losing my job, my apartment was robbed. I told you the part about leaving the door open first, because I find it aggravating when I tell people things like, "my apartment got robbed" and they give me an "Oh, that's terrible!" reaction *before* I tell them it was my fault for doing something that neurotypical people don't do (in this case leaving my apartment door ajar in South Florida).

Eventually I figured out who did it, because they took the cat, too! There were a few guys I had met through a friend, who'd noticed that I left my place unlocked and saw an opportunity. I did end up making a few black friends in Florida, and one of them was this guy named Gabe. The kids who stole my stuff didn't like me, but they really hated Gabe. After nearly cleaning my place out, they actually planted Beautiful Boy in Gabe's apartment complex, knowing I would find him there because of his collar and tag. Thankfully, their plan partially worked, and I found my cat, but it wasn't too hard to figure out that they'd been trying to frame Gabe. I knew it couldn't have been a black person who broke into my house—they didn't take any of my sneakers!

Instead of sticking it out in Florida, I made the decision to get a "fresh start" and leave. I decided to go back to Maine and try to attend college again. To this day, that is a decision I regret. I should not have blamed my problems on geography. When I moved back to Maine, my whole life collapsed, and I turned into someone I look back at and barely recognize.

Fight Night in Bangor

The year 2012 was for me what 2007 was for Britney Spears: a truly disastrous year of self-destruction. Instead of shaving my head bald like Britney, I had put on eighty pounds, gotten in trouble with the law, disrespected my parents, and pretty much given up on life. I was the biggest I had ever been. The weight didn't just affect me physically—it had adverse effects on my mental state.

Whereas an afternoon in Florida in 2011 consisted of going to the gym, an afternoon for me in Bangor, Maine, in 2012 was going to a grocery store, buying a bunch of junk food, and then eating it in my car while listening to talk radio.

There was a girl named Morgan who worked the checkout line at Shaw's, and I thought she was really cute. I chatted her up one day and got her Facebook, but she never accepted my friend request. Most people would take that as a hint and let it drop, but I have a hard time accepting hints that don't make sense to me. If someone rejects me, I not only want them to tell me straight up, I want a detailed explanation. It's an unrealistic expectation I tend to have of people and it gets me into a lot of trouble.

A week later when I was back in her line, I couldn't resist bringing it up to her. "So, you didn't think I'd make a good Facebook friend, huh?" I asked. "Oh, I have a bunch of friend requests just chilling on there," she told me. Again, most people would have taken that as a rejection and moved on, and maybe even I would have a year earlier. But having let go of every ounce of self-discipline I had in life, I wasn't in a state of mind where I could just shake it off. I went outside to my car and just sat there thinking about it, getting more and more rustled. Then, about twenty minutes later, I see Morgan walking outside to her car, holding her uniform like she's leaving for the day. I decided it would be a good idea to follow her in my car. I have no idea what I was thinking would come from this.

Have you ever had someone ignore you, and then you get a strong urge to creep all their social media and just lurk them? I think it was an extreme case of that. And with it being dark outside, I didn't think she would know it was me.

I followed this poor girl all the way out to a rural neighborhood twenty minutes away. Eventually it occurred to me that she knew I was following her because she started driving in circles, so I took off. I still didn't think she could have possibly known it was me following her though. When I got home I looked her up on Facebook again, and she had blocked me. *I still didn't connect the dots!* I just thought, "Oh, that's weird." I didn't think I would hear any more about it, and I definitely didn't realize the seriousness of what I had done.

The next Friday, I got a message on Facebook inviting me to go to a keg party out in the woods. It was like the ultimate gift on a lonely Friday night: this guy was all enthusiastic, telling me there was beer and lots of girls and I needed to come party with them!

It should have seemed too good to be true, and the fact that it was out in the middle of the woods should have been a red flag. But I fell right into their trap. They knew I'd accept an invitation to go do something with people on a Friday night.

Thank God I wasn't alone—I was with Andre, a friend I had made. Andre may have been somewhat using me because he lived in the dorms, and I used to let him crash on my couch. But I was pretty much using him, too. My obsession with black culture at this time was nowhere near finished, and since Andre was black, he'd bring his other black friends over, and I'd have someone to hang and watch music videos with. (The college I attended had a football program, so there were a lot of black guys, but no black girls. 🫤)

So, off we went to this miraculous party, where they just decided to invite extra dudes. When we got there, three guys were standing on the side of the road in a deserted parking lot with nothing around. It wasn't even paved; just a strip of dirt on the side of the road and then woods. I thought, "Oh cool, they're here to meet us and bring us to the party."

When I stepped out of the car, these three goons rushed toward me and yelled, "HEY DIELAWN!" in a tone that was far from friendly. Not until that point did it finally strike me that something was wrong.

They threw me against the car and started beating on me. Then Morgan came out of the woods with a couple of other guys, and now I knew for sure why I was there. She started cursing me out, saying, "What the f*ck is wrong with you? You chased me down with your car! Do you realize how scared I was??" As they continued with blow after blow, she said, "If you ever come in my line again at Shaw's, I'll call security and have you removed!"

While Morgan was yelling at me, she said something that really caught my attention: she called me "fat ass!" 😶

My whole life I have dealt with people that don't like me. I have had every insult in the book thrown at me . . . but I had never been called fat. And with the enemies I've made, if people could have called me fat, they absolutely would have. I really hadn't realized how fat I had gotten; I was the frog in boiling water that doesn't realize he's getting cooked.

I was up against my car with my back turned to them and my arms protecting my face, and they were just ruthlessly pounding my neck and upper back. To try to get them to stop, I yelled, "Okay, okay, I'm sorry!" Andre started backing me up, saying, "All right, he said he's sorry! Let him go!"—but they didn't.

Andre jumped in and started taking some blows himself, which was really brave of him. Now they were beating Andre, (and you can imagine what they were calling him), so I had a second to grab my keys. It must have been some kind of gift from God that I'd actually bought pepper spray a few weeks prior. (I was living in the sticks, and some gas stations sell all those country supplies, so just on a whim I'd picked up a little pepper spray thing and had it on my keychain.) I frantically sprayed it out and it didn't get to me but it got in the air and was enough to get them off me for good. One of the guys tried to come at me again, but another one yelled, "Stop! He's got pepper spray!"

You might think it's not very manly that I didn't try to fight back, or that I had pepper spray. But remember that I am autistic *and* Jewish. If I were just one of those things, I probably wouldn't be a great street fighter. That's just not what I was put on this earth for. When someone challenges me to a debate, that's where you'll see a beat-down. And since we don't live in prehistoric times, which is a better talent to have?

On the way home, Andre was really pissed at me; he had gotten hurt much worse than I had and was bleeding. I didn't know what to do or say; but I was really thankful that I didn't have to go through that kind of thing alone. He advised me, "Don't do that stalker sh*t! This is what happens!"

What I had done was wrong, and I probably deserved what was coming to me. But what if this had been violence toward a female? Not only is violence toward men overlooked, it is often laughed about and encouraged. People say things like, "Oh, he's gonna get his ass beat!"—and no one raises an eyebrow. If we didn't live in a society where we're trying to stamp out every double standard that exists between males and females, then I wouldn't be complaining. But we do live in that society.

On a much sunnier note! Just a reminder to follow me on social media, you won't regret it!

YouTube: Real Dielawn
Twitter: @RealDielawn
Instagram: @RealDielawn
Facebook: Real Dielawn
Snapchat: RealDielawn

Follow me everywhere before you forget!

An awkward middle school photo - with my old cat, Boomer

Remember the ghettoed-out graphic I told you about? 🖤

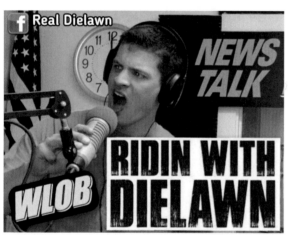

My radio show in 2016

In Utah with my friends Megan and Mick, this still makes me laugh 😁

With Lance Bass! I couldn't wait to make this my Tinder picture!

I should've just let them put this up on the wall!

Peak optics with Dante, Reginald, and Terrance

Me with my biggest fans, accepting the 2015 Spurwink
"Humanitarians of the Year" award

Jordan and I at the Lady Gaga concert!

Brittany and I advertising seat belts, Summer 2009

Anna and I, Fall 2009

I always make sure to get a selfie with the audience!

A Crossroads in My Life

Utah, Fall 2012

Speaking of pepper spray, in October of 2012, shortly after the aforementioned incident where I pepper-sprayed my sister, my parents decided it was time they sent me to a final program to get myself together. They will tell you they gave me a choice of either going to a program in Utah or getting dropped off at a homeless shelter. And they will tell you that they were "very proud" of me for "making the right choice." With all due respect, I felt then and I still feel now that it is utterly ridiculous to call it a choice. First of all, who would ever choose a homeless shelter over being supported financially and emotionally, with a roof over your head? Second, if something isn't a *viable* option, it's not an option. You wouldn't say I have the "option" of punching a cop. You would say: "You can't punch a cop!" Obviously, one literally has the option but to ignore reality in favor of dictionary definitions is just . . . autistic.

I had no concept of Utah other than that it had mountains. It wasn't until chatting with the woman next to me on the plane, (about five minutes before landing) that I found out apparently I was going to "Mormon country." Still, other than Mitt Romney and Glenn Beck, I had no concept of Mormons either. If you have not read *Chasing the Rabbit,* the program was called "At The Crossroads (ATC)" and it was for young guys who needed to grow up. ATC put us up in an apartment with other young men in the city of St. George, Utah, and helped you with "adulting." They helped us get a job, manage money, and be independent. Let me start out by emphasizing that St. George is in southwest Utah, about two hours from Las Vegas. When I tell people I lived in Utah, they assume Salt Lake City, and they always think of winter and snow skiing. No, no, this was the desert—think palm trees and cactuses. 🌵

Walking around, one of my first impressions was, "I can't believe I found a place that's whiter than Maine!" St. George was about the size of my hometown of Portland, Maine, but that was where the similarities ended.

People in St. George were a very different kind of people than I was used to. Everyone was friendly and seemed generally happy and in a good mood most of the time, as opposed to being bitter and having a chip on their shoulder, which is how people in the Northeast can come across. As I got introduced to all the staff members and the guys I would be living and working with in the program, I was shocked at how rational, reasonable, and down-to-earth they all were.

The people I was used to dealing with in every other program or school I had been to operated with the philosophy that every problem could be solved by enforcing more rules. For example, if two people at Zirconia disagreed on what radio station the boom box was set to, the staff would just ban playing music. Or in middle school in Maine, when I asked if I could wait thirty seconds for the kids to clear the hallway so I wouldn't have to be seen going into the special ed room, the prospect of breaking protocol to accommodate the social pressures of being an adolescent was something they couldn't contend with. I apologize to any people in that field who don't fit that description, but that was my experience for eighteen years. If you're different, give yourself a pat on the back, because I think you're the exception, not the rule.

Being in St. George put my whole life in perspective. Growing up around uptight authority figures, I always felt like I must be the crazy one! I assumed the staff members of ATC would be just as brutal, so I went out there fists-up, ready to swing. Once I got to know them and realized that this program was different from the ones I had been to in the past, I realized I could really chill out in St. George. And believe me, at that time in my life that is what I really needed!

When I got to Utah, I was a complete mess. Every ounce of progress I'd made over the years had flown out the window and

I had degenerated into a version of myself that shouldn't have been possible. I was obnoxious and inappropriate. Nasty habits like picking at my skin and smoking cigarettes had come back. And here I was in a program where you basically lived in a house with a bunch of neurotypical guys, most of whom were there for substance abuse or minor criminal issues. To no one's surprise, things didn't go very smoothly at first.

Most of the guys in the program were relatively cool. They were the type of guys I would probably have wanted to hang out with outside of ATC. It's an odd pairing that you commonly see in programs, in high school special ed classes, and other settings. You have the badasses with tattoos and criminal histories and the kids with autism grouped together in one space. It benefits us because they take away the stigma of being in special ed by blurring the lines of what special ed is, almost making it look cool.

Initially there was a lot of friction between me and the other guys in the program. None of them liked me or took me seriously. There was one kid, Amit, who was the coolest five-foot-tall Indian dude you've ever meet. This guy was banging white girls that were a foot taller than he was. He and I got into an argument in front of some of the other guys when I was telling some story about a girl I hooked up with. He started calling me out, saying that he didn't believe I had ever been with a girl before.

Just like getting called a fat-ass, this was new insult territory for me. Plenty of people had thrown shade my way before, but nobody had ever called me a virgin. And Amit wasn't just messing with me, he was being serious. I asked what made him think that and he said, "It's your look, your vibe, just your whole aura, dude! I don't believe you." So in other words, I had regressed so far from where I was that people couldn't believe I had ever been there. Wow, that hit close to home. Yet another splash of cold water that I needed to wake me up.

There was a kid named Sammy, a.k.a. Ramzi, who was also Middle Eastern. He claimed he was a rapper. He and I didn't really get along well either (mostly because I was annoying). I kept telling him we should do a rap battle. He talked a big game about his freestyling skills and claimed that back in his hometown he was "a legend." He didn't take me seriously *at all*. He thought it was funny that I even wanted to challenge him to a battle. Every time I brought it up, he would pretend to laugh it off like I was kidding.

There's a saying in the African-American community, "Don't *talk* about it, *be* about it," and I wasn't kidding. Through my incredible persistence, the same personality trait that made the jail guards in Florida hope I would leave quickly, I finally got Ramzi to agree to a battle. I sat down for four hours and wrote about nine verses of diss rap lyrics. I worked my ass off because I was taking this seriously and wanted to go head-to-head with someone who claimed he was "a legend in his town." I convinced the program to make an event of it, and on the night of the battle, everybody in the program came out to watch.

A dude named Colton, one of the only guys who liked me, played the role of announcing us, much like how they announce wrestlers when they come into the ring. He and three of the other guys were the "judges" to decide who would win the battle.

When the battle started, it was immediately clear that Ramzi had really not taken the challenge seriously and was lying about his skills on the mic. I hit him mercilessly with line after line of clever, lyrical disses, such as:

> You can't stop the humiliation that's about to ensue
> It's time for your shi**y verse — now's your cue

Meanwhile his "verses" were mumbling, incoherent rambles, and during half of them he lost his train of thought mid-sentence. Nobody had expected this! Since he bragged about being a veteran of rap battles, I was the complete underdog. It was like the 2016 primaries: I was Donald Trump and he was Jeb Bush. Nobody could believe how thoroughly I was destroying him, including me! 🤐 This is still on YouTube, by the way, if you search Dielawn vs. King Ramzi. Take special note to see the reactions from the guys behind me while I rap.

Toward the end, I hit him with:

This sh*t is far from a stalemate
Your verbal skills are like that of a primate
Why you always leave the string hangin' out when you menstruate?
I don't know how much more of this I need to dominate
Before you take your Arab ass back to Kuwait!

Everybody screamed and jumped up and down, and I knew I had this sh*t won officially. During his last verse he stumbled over some words and threw his hands up and said, "Ahhh, I don't know, I'm tired."

To his credit, he did give me props and said he was "actually kind of impressed" that I could write. My friend Colton got in a huddle with the other "judges" and then said, "All right ladies and gentlemen, we have a winner. This is by a lot. And the championship goes to DJ Dielawn!"

From that point on, all the guys realized that I was a natural comedian and started to respect me a little more. It always takes something big like that rap battle for me to win people over, so they might possibly like me. Much like the analogy that was made at the boarding school I got kicked out of—that the way I enter social interactions is by busting down the door like a firefighter—I can never just naturally and effortlessly become part of the group. It's exhausting having to work that hard for just a chance at friendship, but that's how my life works.

Fired in Utah

One of my jobs in Utah was a delivery driver for a pizza restaurant. After closing, the drivers would stay and help clean up the kitchen with the assistant manager, who was nineteen years old—chronologically younger than I was. One evening, as I was mopping the floor, I accidentally spilled the entire bucket of water all over the small kitchen. And it wasn't just a single coat of water that had spilled. You could have hydroplaned across that floor.

I didn't know what to do. He didn't know what to do. So, he

told me to grab a mop and start mopping. I was swishing water right and left and it didn't seem to be dissipating. Well, maybe just a little. After fifteen minutes, I asked him, "You think this looks good enough? You think I can leave, or should I keep going?" It looked wet but I'm not an expert at mopping or evaporation, and I wasn't sure what it would look like when it dried.

All I wanted was a yay or nay from my supervisor. He looked right at me and said, "I mean, if you think that looks good, I guess we can take off." —not exactly giving me the straight answer I was asking for.

Back I went mopping for another fifteen minutes or so. Like I said, I have no formal training in the custodial arts, so again I asked, "Is this good enough?" And again, he gave me a vague answer that I couldn't interpret as a yes or a no. I have autism. When it comes to instructions on the job, I need black and white. Gray instructions don't exist in my world. My brain cannot process ambiguous information. If you give me anything other than black or white, my brain virtually shuts down. He said, "Man, if you think that's good, we'll take off."

The next morning, when we arrived for work, the floor looked dreadful, and I was fired. And of course, I got to find out *as* I was getting fired that there had been other issues too, just none that had been brought to my attention! 😦 The wet floor had merely been the final of many invisible straws.

As it turned out, I hadn't been learning the menu quick enough and there were other little issues bothering my boss and my coworkers that were so subtle, I'm having a hard time remembering what they were so I can describe them to you, the reader. I had just been getting under people's skin and coming across the wrong way—*but not a word had been spoken to me.* No one told me there were any issues or concerns at all. That employers are allowed to do this is so outrageous that I personally don't see how it is legal. An employee, let alone one with a disability, should be given the chance to correct their mistakes, one hundred percent of the time.

This is just one example of the complex miscommunications that can arise in the workplace. Looking back at the jobs where I did disclose my disability, versus the ones where I didn't, there is almost no discernible difference in my experiences. Sure, they'll pay my autism plenty of lip service up front. They'll act like they are going to be the most accommodating workplace in America. But at the end of the day people go by what they feel, not by what they know. Even the times when I've told my boss and my coworkers about my disability, if one month later, they didn't feel like I had a disability, it was as if I didn't even tell them. I have had a couple of jobs since where the managers did exactly what this manager in Utah should have done, which was sit me down and say, "People have been saying X, I've seen you doing Y, I need you to do Z." This aversion that we have to delivering even mildly bad news to one another may seem kind, but it is unhelpful in the long run.

The Job Workshop, 2013

There was a guy in ATC named Kyle who was kind of an all-star student of the program. Kyle had come way before me, and now he had a job, his own apartment and a super-hot, blonde Utah girlfriend. The biggest emphasis of the program was getting a job, so once a month Kyle would do a "job workshop" where he would walk us through the process of getting a job and give us some leads for places that were hiring. The first time I went, I thought it was awesome. His advice was great; it was real and down-to-earth. He said a lot of things I knew, and some things that I didn't—like, that 90 percent of places don't call references.

It wasn't your dad's advice on getting a job—it was real world advice. I thought to myself, "If I wasn't such a mess and had my sh*t together, I could totally see myself doing this."

Fast-forward seven months. I had my sh*t together a little more, not all the way together, but I was getting it together. I was doing better in the program. Most importantly, I had earned people's respect.

I had recently been fired from a job at Staples but then got a job at Applebee's the same day. Before that, I had gotten a job at Office Max, but it turned out they were closing the store almost immediately after I was hired. That situation was particularly disappointing because in the second interview one of the managers said, "I think we've got a star waiting in the wings." He literally said that! He may have even used the word, "superstar." And then they closed the effing store. That's the kind of luck I usually have in life. If I'm not screwing up on my own, then bad things happen anyway. Either way, I'm not winning.

I also nailed a job at St. George Shuttle. I worked there for just one day, but it didn't work out because it was across town and I didn't have reliable transportation to be there every day at 7:00 a.m. I also landed a job at Harmon's, a luxury grocery store in St. George. I worked in their deli for two weeks and didn't really like it. I had the Staples job at the same time, so I just kept that and quit the Harmon's job. There were a few other jobs that weren't interesting enough for me to talk about, so I won't bore you.

Suffice it to say, I had earned a reputation for getting jobs like a beast. I decided I wanted to share my expertise and said to the people who ran the program, "How about I do the job workshop? I won't do a workshop on how to keep jobs, I'm not qualified for that, but I could damn sure do a workshop about how to get jobs." They let me give it a try. I met with Kyle about it. This was one of the most thrilling moments of my entire time in the ATC program. It doesn't seem like a big deal now, but it was a big deal then. From that first time I had gone to his workshop seven months before, I had thought, "Maybe someday, if I succeed in this program and Kyle doesn't do the workshop anymore, I'll be up there"—and now, here I was, sitting with Kyle as he turned over the keys to me!

Kyle did a thorough job with his version of the workshop, but I took it to another level. I would do research and print out articles that corroborated all the advice I was giving the other guys. One week I told them about the "hidden job market"—(did you know that 80 percent of jobs go unadvertised?) Kyle had printed out all these tips and guidelines and advice. It was like two pages' worth of advice, bullet points, walking you through the do's and don'ts of a job interview and things like that. I was getting to edit and revise it based on my experiences and my opinions. He had in his notes, "It is a good idea to put on cologne and smell nice for a job interview," but then he wrote, *"(No Axe)."* I took issue with that because I'm a fan of Axe, especially that chocolate axe—the "Dark Temptation." If you tell me that's not good stuff, you're just being elitist. I changed it to *"(load up the Axe)."* 😜

It was thrilling to be able to say whatever I wanted to say and do it with authority! It brought my level of respect to a place that no one, including me, foresaw me reaching when I arrived in Utah as a total not-so-hot mess. We would have a group meeting in the program every night, and the night when I announced I would be taking over Kyle's workshop, I told everyone this was the passing of the torch, "like when Madonna kissed Britney!" (Can't ever miss that chance to throw in a pop music reference.) 😊

I did several workshops, and everyone agreed that they were a huge success. I felt I was really turning a corner in my life and realized I liked helping others.

Eighty Pounds in Eight Months

The job workshop was great, but the real turning point of my life in Utah was my decision to once again take the steering wheel and start caring about my physical fitness. I hadn't realized how bad it was—I had gotten up to 230 pounds, and I just thought I was a little chubby. I absolutely couldn't see how fat I was when I looked in the mirror, it was like reverse anorexia.

Looking back at this time, it's shocking to me that I was able to attract girls at all when I was fat. There were a few girls I met, however, who were brave enough to tell me explicitly that they were rejecting me because I was too fat. I greatly appreciate those girls who told me the truth, because that was what I needed, and that was who I needed it from. Anytime I'm not interested in a girl because of her weight, I remember the courage of those few girls, and I pay it forward. 😉

I started going to the gym every single day and eating like a saint. Once I put my mind to something . . . I really feel bad for that thing. When you have only recently put on weight, it's easier to take it off. So from March to November 2013, I lost eighty pounds in eight months.

I had a perfect situation, because when I arrived in Utah I was at my max weight, so naturally everyone assumed that I had looked like that all my life. Especially since I was such a disaster, it fit with my appearance. No one realized that I hadn't always been so fat. Throughout my life my weight has gone up and down, but I had never been anywhere close to the blimp I was in 2012.

I couldn't stand to let people think this was some miracle like they'd watch on *The Oprah Winfrey Show*, and I knew that's what people thought they were witnessing with me. They thought I was like some extreme weight loss hero, when in reality losing weight you have only had for a year is *not* the same as going from being fat all your life to having a six-pack.

Apparently in those early days when I first started going back to the gym, I had been flailing around loudly on the treadmill. I was so out of shape and not used to running that I was way too high up on the machine, and my feet were banging against the plastic. With my headphones on, I never realized how much noise I was making. One day Mo, this sixty-year-old biker guy with huge muscles and long hair, came over to tell me that people at the gym were calling me "Thumper." He then proceeded to tell me all the things I was doing wrong in my workouts and told me that if I listened to his advice, he would get me into shape. You can imagine how I reacted to this—I basically had a b*tch fit. I never asked for his advice so I saw it as an attack, even though he was really being pretty altruistic, giving it to me straight when no one else had the courage to do so.

They say at the gym, 50 percent of the workout is showing up. As the months went by, Mo saw me continuing to show up day after day, and eventually we became friendly. He said when he met me he never imagined I had it in me to stick to it and go all the way with my weight loss. He came over to me one day and said, "Let me tell you, kid, you are one of the top five people in this entire gym, and if you keep going, you're gonna be number one." There was a wall at the gym with people's before and after pics, and he told me I should be up on that wall.

But I couldn't just accept the praise. I pushed back and said, "No, no, no you don't understand. I wasn't always like this!" and gave him my whole story. I always have to explain myself to people. Why couldn't I just accept the compliments? Let them put me on parade and treat me like a local hero? It's this need I have to always be completely understood by everybody, even when it's against my own best interests.

Nevertheless, even with me counter-signaling my own success, my physical transformation earned me a lot of respect from everyone in the program. And the change was more than physical—during those months of weight loss, I became a truly different person.

For example, there was a kid in the program named Zack who had gotten there in April of that year. When he met me, he met a fat, messy-looking kid who smoked cigs, picked at his skin and started arguments with everybody in sight. Understandably, he wanted nothing to do with me. By September, he requested me as a roommate, and we became good friends. He even helped me install a new sound system when I got my car out there.

By December 2013, I had reached all of my fitness goals. I remember looking in the mirror and thinking, "This is what I always wished I looked like." It was pretty great, but I was inexplicably somewhat disappointed that the journey was over. For the last eight months, every week I had lost more and more weight, and it had really given me something to live for. It was kind of like, have you ever gone on vacation, and the day you leave ends up being more exciting than when you actually get there?

When I had gotten my car a few months back, a lot of guys had said to me, "If you had the money for a car, why didn't you just get your own place?" Splurging on my own apartment instead of a car seemed absurd to me. I knew I needed the help of the program, I liked the structure it provided, and I liked being part of something. Most people on the spectrum love structure; we crave it more than almost anything. For me, I like it because my mind has such a hard time prioritizing and organizing my time in our crazy, fast-paced world. Structure gives me an escape from that mental burden because someone else is deciding things for me. A lot of guys were bothered by the idea of being under supervision and having people help them run their lives. I feel like that "you're-not-the-boss-of-me" attitude is a very neurotypical thing. I like being bossed around (not in a weird way), I like having people to answer to and having clear expectations set for me. Neurotypical people seem to love the idea of "being your own boss." That's an alien way of thinking to me.

Zack had moved out of the program, and now I was just left with Harley, an obese snitch who refused to get a job. I started getting really lonely and feeling like it was time to move on from the Fourplex, which was where everyone lived when they first joined the program. ATC had another location, the Triplex in downtown St. George, which was for the more advanced kids in the program who needed less staff supervision. I had been working with a guy named Magnum as my colleague since I got there. (Your colleague was basically like your ed-tech in the program.) Magnum was great and really understood me, but we'd gotten sick of each other, and I made the tough decision to switch colleagues to Jason, another guy I got along well with. Jason was also the colleague of a guy named Jordan.

Jordan was a black gay guy who had arrived that summer. Like me, he was a huge Lady Gaga fan. He also loved Madonna, and not just her old stuff! (When you meet somebody who knows her new stuff, that's a real Madonna fan.) So when Jason told me I could move to the Triplex if I wanted to room with Jordan, I was pretty excited.

Gay Friends and Gay Club Music

Going through these different phases, where I make friends according to my special interest, could be compared to a tourist passing through an area. A tourist who's visiting for a few years though—so maybe like a student studying abroad. I was over my interest in black culture, so I was thinking to myself, "What culture should I travel to now? What crowd should I target to try and be part of?" My next ambition happened to end up being gay guys.

Being friends with gay guys was never something I had considered before, but mostly because they had never liked me. They had always been very unfriendly and dismissive toward me, and I had always felt like it was because I wasn't good-looking enough for them to take me seriously. It's not any different than a straight guy and a pretty girl. Looks can be a motivating force for friendship, it doesn't mean the friendship is not legitimate. As men, despite what Hollywood would make you believe, we are interested in more than just sex. We are interested in getting to know people we're attracted to, and it's no different with gay men. Now that I was legitimately in-shape and good-looking, I thought maybe that opened up a door.

Just like the way I got into black culture, the big factor here was the music. I'd had this very specific taste in pop music my whole life, and I never quite found anyone else who shared it. I always wondered who else was listening to these female pop stars, because even most girls would say my music was too girly for them! I just love hearing women sing to me, that's all it is. I would say 90 percent of the time I'd rather hear a girl sing than a guy. Ever since I was a little kid I've always thought female singers are just better. And it makes sense! It's like, that's what I like to look at, so that's what I like to listen to. I never understood why every other straight guy doesn't feel the same way. Or maybe they do behind closed doors, and that's who's listening to all these female artists!

But when I met Jordan I finally realized there is a group of people out there with my taste in music . . . gay black guys!!! The first day I moved in, he had Lady Gaga's "Applause" blasting through the whole apartment. That was my favorite song at the time, (and maybe of all time). If you don't know it, and want to hear what I'm talking about, go YouTube it real quick. 😊 "Applause" was from Lady Gaga's album *ArtPop*, which was my favorite album then, and Jordan knew every word to every track on it. Much like how Mark was the first friend I'd ever had that I could talk about the Billboard charts with, Jordan was the first friend who shared my exact taste in pop music like this. With music being how I bond with people, this was a huge deal. He explained to me that what I like is basically "gay club music." I loved that I finally had a name for what I had been drawn to my whole life. And I didn't care what group it was, I was thrilled to find out there *was* a group of people out there who shared my musical taste.

Whenever I identify a group of people that I feel like I can fit in with, I start adjusting myself to be like that group. Some might see that as negative, but I say it's simple assimilation. Jordan and I hung out sometimes, and my work was right next to his, so I would bring him to work every morning, and we'd take snapchat videos blaring songs off of *ArtPop*. With my general lack of social intuition, I probably took it too far trying to show how cool I thought he was and making it obvious I wanted to be friends. I even knew it at the time, but having someone I could jam out with to *recent* Madonna songs? (like "Girl Gone Wild" or "4 Minutes," if you care) Come on, there was no way I was going to be able to hide how cool I thought this guy was. Looking back, I'm sure now if I had to redo it, I could keep it a lot more cool than I could back then, and he might have hit me up more if I hadn't been so enthusiastic.

I never realized how much I had in common with most gay guys; they even eat the same foods that I like to eat. I get my taste in food from my mom—I'm very much a food snob. And because I was cursed with terribly slow metabolism, I have to try and eat healthy. That was another thing I never felt like I could relate to other straight guys over. They'd be drinking Mountain Dew and eating a family-sized bag of Cheetos while I'm drinking Crystal Light and ordering salads with vinaigrette dressing. But then I moved in with Jordan and I looked in his kitchen cupboard and saw all the same stuff that I buy.

Gay guys also usually like things clean, which is another reason I wanted to live with him. I've been in a lot of gay guys' apartments since then (I know that doesn't sound good, but whatever, I have) and they're *always* immaculate. I had long been grossed out by the way other straight guys kept their places. But I don't think it's even a straight guy thing, because I've been in a lot of girls' apartments, and Lord knows, they're messy too. So maybe it's just a straight person thing. Since Jordan was my first gay friend, you might be asking, how did I know these things were characterstics of gay people in general? But that's exactly how I did know, because I compared Jordan to every straight friend I'd ever had, and the differences were unmistakable. With the cleanliness, the food thing, and most of all the music thing—all these things added up had me really feeling like I'd found a new identity. I probably flew too close to the sun with it, but we'll get to that later.

Across the street from the Jimmy John's in St. George where I worked at the time was the Dixie Regional Medical Center. They had this stand in the lobby where I would go to get breakfast. The food at this hospital was anything but hospital food. You would've thought it came straight from Panera Bread. But because it was this stand inside the lobby that nobody knew about, it was crazy cheap. I would get this yogurt bowl with berries, granola, and honey for $2.50. I told Jordan he had to try the food there. I also wanted him to go because guess who ran the stand—a very friendly and flamboyant gay man. Well, technically I didn't know! But he'd make all kinds of extra conversation with me about where I worked, where I was from, etc., and I wanted Jordan to confirm my suspicions. I'd never been hit on by a gay guy before, and I've got to say it was pretty thrilling. This is my logic: gays are like the experts on guys. They're men that like other men SO much that they said, "You know what—screw what society thinks, screw what my parents think, I have to have THAT." Obviously I like it if a girl hits on me, but they do it in a way that's much more subtle and muted. Plus, girls are supposed to be attracted to guys. When a gay guy hits on you, it somehow feels more validating, like he's saying, "Wow, THIS is why I'm gay."

So I went in there with Jordan and the guy does his usual extremely friendly banter toward me and when I ordered my usual yogurt bowl, he grabs this giant bowl and puts like half the container of yogurt in there, and charges me the same price of $2.50. As we're walking out I said to Jordan, "So, you think he's gay?" And he goes, "Oh f*ck yeah! And if I had ordered that I'm pretty sure I would've gotten like a fraction of what you got!" I had always wondered incessantly where I was on the attractiveness scale. I felt like I couldn't see myself objectively. Now that I was being hit on by gay guys, I felt like I had arrived, like I was officially hot. 🔥

So we had a fun couple of months hanging out, but Jordan was one of these kids that was dying to get out of the program, so he got his job to transfer him up to Salt Lake City.

Jordan had this shirt he had ordered off LadyGaga.com, and the entire shirt was the cover of her album *ArtPop*. On his last day, I offered to take him around to do any errands he needed to do for his move, but on the condition that he had to wear the *ArtPop* shirt everywhere we went. (If you take a sec to Google "ArtPop," you'll be able to appreciate this on another level.)

We went to Target, and we were being rung up by this cute cashier. I was talking to her about his Lady Gaga shirt and trying to flirt with her to gauge the temperature, and maybe ask for her number. As we were walking out, Jordan pointed out that she wasn't into the conversation. He said, "I'm pretty good at reading people, and when you said something, she'd be like 'Ha, ha, NO.'"

I was surprised because I thought that it went better than that! I'd been confident and convinced myself it went well. In that moment I thought about what happened and how he said he was good at reading people. As you mature, there are moments that open your eyes and mark a turning point. This was a big moment for me. I replayed the conversation in my head and thought about what the girl's facial expressions had been. I thought to myself, there's no reason I couldn't have read that situation just as easily as he did—maybe I just need to open my eyes to what's actually happening, instead of trying to spin it into something it isn't.

I know this may not seem like a big deal, but it clicked with me. Having Asperger's, I wasn't born with the ability to read people. It's something I have to learn as I go. It never stops being something I need to work on. It's as if my whole life is like a school for social skills, but I'm never quite graduating.

Jordan's leaving didn't seem real to me until I saw the U-Haul truck, and he was packing all his stuff. It had been fun making friends with him, being his roommate and bonding over music. I said a few nice words to him before he left. I said, "Hey man, I've really enjoyed hanging out with you these past couple of months and getting to know you. You've honestly been one of my best friends, and I'm really going to miss you."

Let me just say this, there are two kinds of crying. There's *giving in to the cry*, where you're sobbing, and there's *holding in the cry*, like fighting back the tears. The first kind is NEVER acceptable for a man in public, unless *maybe* you're watching your child being born. On RARE occasions, the second kind is acceptable for a man, as long as you completely hold it back. It can actually make you look manly, like you're strong enough to fight the temptation. 💪

I was doing the second kind as I was saying goodbye to Jordan. He noticed that I had tears in my eyes, and he started laughing like, "Oh my God!"—not like he was making fun of me—more like he was surprised and thought it was endearing. As soon as he left, I went to my room and locked the door, and then I cried for real—just for a minute, but it felt good—not like a painful cry—more like a healthy release cry. It felt nice to care about something. I'd really connected with Jordan over my first and foremost love, my interest in pop music, and he was the first friend I'd been able to share that with.

The good news was that I knew I'd be seeing him again at the end of the summer, because for my birthday that year I told my parents all I wanted was two tickets to see Lady Gaga when she came to Salt Lake City for her *ArtRave* tour. Until then, I felt like there was a strong possibility Jordan would be expecting me to be hitting him up all the time wanting to talk. But I'd just had that epiphany remember, when he told me he was good at reading people? I made a call that I felt was a real sign of progress for my social skills. I decided that since I hadn't been able to keep it much of a secret how cool I thought he was, the best thing I could do until *ArtRave* was not talk to him at all. Not even once.

About a month later, guess who I got a Snapchat from! He said, "Listen to Sharon Doorson, 'High on Your Love'." (If you want to hear a top-tier gay club song, go Google that right now.) To have someone be able to recommend me a song that I knew was going to be *exactly* what I liked, was just too cool. And it wouldn't have happened if I'd been annoying after he left. In my life of learning social skills from scratch, that moment felt like a real step forward.

Sarah Staheli

One of the few girls I encountered who was brave enough to tell me I was too fat was Sarah Staheli. I had added her on Facebook back in April 2013 and tried talking to her, but I got totally blown out. She stopped responding to me and then finally told me I should go to the gym. I told her I *was* going to the gym, and she said, "Well, apparently you aren't working hard enough there!" Rough, but much-needed!

Fast-forward to January 2014. I am not sure how, but somehow Sarah was on my Snapchat. I sent a selfie of myself to a bunch of people on my friends list and must have included her. A couple of days later I got a Snapchat pic from her that was just her legs in a bubble bath, and it said, "What are you up to?" We started snapping, and it took me a minute to remember who she was. I could tell that she, however, definitely didn't remember who I was. If you look at the "before" and "after" picture of me (see the photos section), just imagine being a girl who had met the "before," and now was meeting the "after!" I was pretty much unrecognizable, and now she was attracted to me and flirting with me without realizing she had rejected me nine months prior! This was like something out of a sitcom; but the question was, should I tell her who I was? Or just let her think I was a different person? I'm sure you can guess which one I did. I had to tell her! "Oh, jeez," I thought. "Am I gonna regret this? Is she about to block me as soon as I jog her memory?" But she barely even remembered me, thank God!

Sarah invited me over that Friday night. I got off work and got ready faster than I've ever gotten ready before. She lived in a rural neighborhood out in Santa Clara with huge-ass houses. From the moment I stepped out of the car, the whole night was like something out of a movie. Her neighborhood was covered in snow, even though there was none in St. George. There was a full moon, so it was dark and bright at the same time, with the snow all shiny from the moonlight; it felt like I had passed through the wardrobe into Narnia. I was on the phone with her as I walked through her yard, trying to figure out where her window was. I worried, "What if her parents see a random guy walking through their yard?!" I can't lie, it definitely added to the adrenaline rush. Her room was in the basement, and it was one of those houses where the basement was halfway underground, so her window was on the ground level. Finally, I saw this open window, and she was waving at me—I thought "Could this be any more cinemagic?"

Thank God I was skinny by then because she had to squeeze me through the little half-window and have me jump down into her room! The moment I landed, I came face to face with her, and wow! She was even hotter in person. If I had closed my eyes and pictured "my type," it would have been a picture of Sarah. She was tall (exactly my height, five foot nine, which is perfect for a girl), she was thin with long legs, and she was blonde with a super-cute, friendly face. You know how sometimes you can tell within the first five minutes if a date is going well? This was one of those.

Back in 2007, my mom and I had seen a comedian named Dan Levy at a club in Portland, Maine. I had bought his album after the show, and it had been living in an old case of CDs I just happened to bring with me to Utah. When I got there, I was bored one day so I dusted off the album and listened to it. It turned out the album was recorded in Utah. As soon as you pop in the CD, he says "Hey, what is going on Utah? Yes, I love it here, mountains and Mormons, that's what I like!" All the jokes on the CD were suddenly relevant to where I was! You can't write coincidences like that. So I had the album on my phone and I thought it would be good to break the ice with Sarah. Dan Levy talks about how every girl in Utah is married and says, "What, you're eighteen!?" She was eating it up, doing that thing where she was laughing with her head on my chest and everything. Not only did she look perfect, but her personality was a ten too.

She was really smart, with a great sense of humor. Like I said before, a sense of humor is one of those things every person on earth claims to have, but do they? I would define it as someone who laughs at things other people don't notice.

We watched two movies on her iPhone while lying on her bed and making out. One of them was a random British indie comedy on Netflix; it had really dry British humor, and she actually got it! Hands down, this was one of the best first dates I had ever been on.

Right before I left, I picked her up and made out with her before climbing back out through her window. I felt like I was in an old Taylor Swift music video. It was like a high school fairytale that I never quite had, (not very many of them, anyway). It was making up for more lost time and then some.

The ride home and the next day had me feeling like I was in a trance. But as you can imagine, I can't have a date go this well without paying a price. Now I was petrified that things wouldn't continue to go well. How was I going to keep this girl in my life? That Sunday, I got a really good sign: she liked one of my pictures on Instagram! You can laugh, but is that or is that not a sign that someone is still into you? There was a guy in the program I had made friends with named Mick, and I had never met anyone with better advice on what to say to girls than this guy. We used to go to the gym together and we would Snapchat girls on my phone. As we lifted weights we would be debating what the next thing we should say was. Thank God I had his help, because I wouldn't have gotten a second and third date with Sarah without Mick coaching me on what to say.

Ever since I had quit smoking and gotten in shape, chewing gum had become my new habit. I carried all different kinds of gum with me, figuring it was a much healthier vice than cigs. Trident Layers was my favorite, and during Christmas they had a limited edition of Candy Cane gum. It was the bomb. I brought a bunch of it with me on that second date, and Sarah loved it. We just hung out in her room all night, chewing Candy Cane gum and making out; it was all pepperminty and perfect.

By this point I was wondering how far I could take this. I would have loved to turn it into a relationship, but as I said, Sarah was not only a pretty blonde, but she was also highly intelligent. In my experience, intelligence plays just as big of a role in how diffi-cult girls are to attract as their looks do—the smarter a girl is, the more of a challenge she is. So, even being the hopeless romantic that I am, I never actually thought a relationship with someone like her would happen. In fact, I had a strong feeling she was just using me for sexual stuff, so Mick and I tested it out: he told me to tell her I didn't want to do anything the next time we hung out. I told her, and she replied, "Nothing?" I said, "Yeah," and she just sent back "😶."

There was my answer. It wasn't hard to figure out what was going on here: Sarah came from a Mormon family, and lived a Mormon life, in a Mormon community. I was a mysterious twen-ty-two-year-old who didn't know anybody in her world, so she could sneak me in late at night and do things with me without anybody in her life ever finding out. She was never going to be my girlfriend, but I was happy to be that guy in the meantime!

If I thought it was hard getting the second date, the third date really looked like it wouldn't happen. It took an agonizing month's worth of playing it just right, keeping her interest but not coming on too strong, and hours on hours spent with Mick deliberating on what to say to Sarah to miraculously end up on a third date with her. We met up at the movies this time, to see *Ride Along* with Ice Cube and Kevin Hart. We had a nice time, and after the third date is supposed to be when things start to happen, but just as things were looking like they were going good, I'm not sure what happened. It just fizzled out.

Months later, Mick got to meet her, which was cool after all the time he had spent helping me. We had gone to work out at Gold's Gym, which I knew was her gym, but I honestly wasn't thinking she would be there. But holy sh*t, there she was! Mick and I were trying to figure out how to make it look like I wasn't there to stalk her. When she walked out the door, we were standing outside the entrance. Mick yelled "Sarah!" and she turned around and had a friendly conversation with him. A lot of girls would be all awkward and standoffish in a moment like that. After just that short interaction, Mick said, "I know what you mean now about her personality! She has a swag about her."

It could have been better, but that I was able to get three dates with her, I counted as a major success. That August, I saw on Instagram that she'd gotten a boyfriend. She had told me of course, that she wasn't into relationships. I wasn't surprised, but I couldn't resist messaging her and saying, "Remember when you told me you didn't do relationships? 🙂 "

There's a Yiddish expression that goes, "The way it begins is the way it ends." First she blocked me on social media and blew me off, and a year-and-a-half later she blocked me all over again. And I'm still blocked to this day. Though I did go on another account and looked her up, and true to the Dan Levy routine, she got married at eighteen.

Gay Guys and Blond Hair

In June of 2014, I moved out of ATC housing and into student housing at Dixie State University, which for some reason you didn't have to be a student to live in. Living on campus was great, because now I was in a community surrounded by people my age; it was impossible not to make friends!

With Jordan gone, my mission was to make friends with more gay guys who liked pop music—and if they could be black, that'd be ideal. There was a group of gays that lived in the apartments across the street from me; I went over and hung out with them one night, and they were blasting a new song by the girl group Danity Kane called "Lemonade." This was a fairly obscure pop song that I had been jamming to for weeks now, but I didn't think anybody else knew about it! I thought, "This is amazing—I *have* to be accepted into this circle."

I had always dreamed about one day dying my hair blond, but I never felt enough confidence in my physical shape to pull it off. Here I was in the summer of 2014; I had reached all my fitness goals, and I was living in Utah where everyone is blond anyway! I thought if I was ever going to go blond, now was the time.

I came back from the salon all excited to show off my new blond hair to everyone. I honestly didn't know that blond hair was a thing that a lot of gay men do. I was thinking I wanted to look like Zack Morris from *Saved by the Bell* or Niall from *One Direction*. I had been wondering, however, in the back of my mind, if I was going too far with this new metro-sexual persona I had taken on. I had found that I had a lot in common with gay guys, but with my style, my mannerisms, and my driving around bumping Lady Gaga, was I crossing the line into coming off like I *was* a gay guy? But I kind of pushed the thought away, all in the name of "being myself."

I was living in a shared room with another guy also named Dylan, and I walked in and asked what he thought of my hair. Then, wanting to brag a little, I told him I was going to hang out with this group of gay guys I had met. He said, "You're not gay?"

Whoa. It was the first time anybody had really said that to me, and it was very alarming to hear. I would say it was like a splash of cold water, but it was more like an ice bucket challenge.

"What made you think I was gay?" I said.

"The way you talk—the way you act—just, like everything you do."

To hear somebody verbalize what I had been suspecting in the back of my mind, felt like a curtain had been pulled back on my innermost, private thoughts. It was so unnerving how immediately real it became. It's not so much that I cared about being seen as gay—it's that I don't like people thinking I'm something I'm not. Just like with the weight loss thing, I don't want to be misunderstood, even if it's a good thing.

"Oh well, no, I'm not," I said. But of course, it didn't matter.

The point is that he thought I was gay. He probably would have had more respect for me if I had been. As a straight guy, you are not supposed to come off as gay. (Don't blame me, blame the culture we live in) If you're straight and you come off as gay, you will be mocked and disrespected. However, if you *are* gay, then there's nothing wrong with that. So let me see if I understand this . . . if you're straight and you come off as something people respect, then people don't respect you. Can someone explain that logic to me? Again, don't blame me, blame the culture—go out there and do some activism—I'm just telling you how it is.

I tried to shake it off and go outside, and what do you know, the whole crew of gay guys was hanging out at the barbeque pit by my complex's pool. My goal was to go out there and brush it off my shoulders, but dropping things is not my gift. I made it about thirty seconds before I brought it up.

"Somebody told me they thought I was gay, did you guys think that too?" I inquired. I had on a button-up blue shirt, and I had the top three buttons undone Hasselhoff-style to show off my chest (which I had working my ass off on), along with the blond hair spiked up, and almost-skinny gray jeans. Jazmine, who was a half-black transgender girl and kind of the leader of the group, clapped her hands and said, "Dylan, hunny, I'm sorry to tell you this, but you're flaming right now—You're flaming in that outfit."

Everyone started laughing and agreeing, and maybe I should have just laughed it off, but I was still very unsure about myself. I was trying so hard to find my identity. To me this was much deeper than just the outfit I was wearing. I was clearly upset, and started doing what I do when I'm upset—arguing.

Ronald, a Hispanic gay guy who lived with Jazmine, tried to talk to me. He was a smart, nice guy, and he told me, "Look, no offense, but sometimes the music you play and the things you talk about—it's just, you do a lot of the same things I would do, that's all."

I appreciated that he broke it down for me; it was the kind of thing Anna used to do. I said "Okay, I get that."

Frankly, it made me feel better that he compared himself to me. I liked that I wasn't alone; I liked that there was a group of people who did things like I did, even if we had a different sexual preference. Two seconds later, I spotted some speakers, but nobody was playing music. I asked if I could connect my phone, and I put on "Can't Get You Out of My Head" by Kylie Minogue. If you YouTube that one, you'll probably recognize it. Just imagine going from having people explain to me why I was coming off gay, and then the second that conversation is over, playing that song. 😄

Ronald said, "See!" pointing to the speaker, "You see what I'm talking about?" I thought it was hilarious, almost like something out of a sitcom, and maybe that was partly why I did it, but I also just really wanted to play some Kylie Minogue. 🎵

I never ended up being truly accepted into this group, but my semi-friendship with them hung on for another few weeks until an incident on my birthday when everything blew up.

By early July, these guys had already been hitting me up less and less, and I was worried I might be losing my friendship with them. I went over and casually mentioned that it was my birthday weekend, and they told me, "Come over Friday night and we'll party." So my birthday was really my Hail Mary pass, this was my last shot to try to fit in with this group, and be a part of this social circle.

Everything seemed to be going okay: one guy, Chris (picture a twenty-year-old version of Cam on *Modern Family)* had bought me a big bottle of Absolut vodka for a present, so we were all sipping on that and the night was pretty uneventful. Fast-forward to around 4 a.m. and it was just Chris and I left in the apartment. I was going through a lot of identity issues at that time and struggling to figure out who I was, and Chris had been acting like he was my friend more than any of the other guys, so I thought he would be a good ear for me. Earlier that night, he had been going through my Facebook on his laptop (which I love when people do), and as you go further back in my profile pictures, you notice the clothes getting more and more urban. I had told him, "Yeah, I used to be pretty hood," and he said, "I know—I'm sensing a theme here . . ." which I found hilarious. Now that the night was winding down, I drunkenly started ranting about some of my deepest thoughts.

I was going on about how I had gravitated toward black culture because I liked that black guys had a certain swag, a certain presentation, and way of carrying themselves. I told him I felt the same was true about gay guys and that I had a hard time relating to other straight white guys because I felt like they didn't have a strong style. With most white guys, it's more a lack thereof, like this bland, vanilla thing. It frustrated me that I couldn't identify with that because I'm not a bland person; I like style, and I like to have a certain flavor to me. I had been drunk-venting for what felt like twenty minutes, and I looked over to the other side of the couch and saw that Chris had passed out while I'd been talking. Embarrassed, I got up and walked home.

That's what really happened. But as I found out the next day, Chris decided to go around telling everyone that I had let him perform oral sex on me. Yup, that's right. I went over there as soon as I heard, very frustrated and confrontational, and I demanded that he tell people the truth. Everyone was right there in his apartment, and Jazmine said, "Dylan, it's okay if you're gay – nobody cares!" I rolled my eyes at hearing this again, and then I paused for a second and said, "Is it okay if I'm straight?" Because that was the real question: *was it okay with Jazmine, Ronald, and Chris if I like girls, and I also happen to like the music I like, and the clothes I wear? Was it okay if I was myself?* To which she dismissively replied, "Yeah, obviously if you're straight then . . . whatever," not at all considering my point, (which I thought was pretty profound!)

What really infuriated me was how insidious this was of Chris to do. He knew this idea was already in people's heads about me, and all he had to do was say something happened late at night when we'd gotten drunk, and it'd be over for me. He knew nobody would believe me over him, and he was right. It's that classic dirty trick people play where the person that's been known for a long time gets believed over the new guy. I've seen it many times in my many workplaces.

There was also the fact that, in talking to a lot of gay guys since, I've learned that there are far more "straight" guys out there than one would imagine who will accept this "favor" from another guy, with the rationale that "head is head." I personally find that thinking degenerate: I feel that it shouldn't be about the act; it should be about who is performing the act. I wouldn't even want that from a girl I'm not attracted to! 😶

Armed with both of these factors, Chris knew he had this very plausible story he could sell to everyone that would be the final nail in my friendship coffin. I was baffled at the time as to why he wanted to do this to me. I realized later that he had liked me, and in his mind, he thought I must be gay, or at least curious, so he took my insisting that I'm straight as a rejection of him personally. I understand how that feels, I've been rejected and sometimes it hurts so much that you want to hurt the person back.

It still sucked though, because why couldn't they just believe me? I became very argumentative and started addressing Chris right on. As he stood there I saw this smirk in his eyes like he knew exactly what he did, and he knew that I was screwed. It started to get very heated, because I wouldn't drop it, I kept pushing the issue. In my mind I always feel like I can get people to believe the truth, and I have a very hard time accepting that oftentimes the truth is no defense.

The audience for this argument included Kaitlin, who was Chris's roommate and best friend, so you can guess whose side she was on. During the midst of all the arguing, she went out onto the porch and walked back a few steps. Then I saw her wag her finger as she called me through the door like, "Dylan, come here—I want to show you something," thinking she was going to trick me into coming outside.

Now, if I had gone out there, she was probably going to physically assault me, and if I defended myself she would have called the police on me. Or she might have even hit herself and then called everyone outside and said I'd hit her. If this had happened to 2008 Dylan, I absolutely would have fallen for it and gone out there. Thank God by 2014 I had enough savvy to just squint my eyes at her and say, "I don't think so." As you can imagine, this really pissed her off for two reasons. For one, I was basically rejecting her—she was pretending to seduce me and I said no. And two, I had outsmarted her, her attempt to entrap me had backfired. With steam coming out of her ears, she stormed back inside, put her finger in my face, and said, "Don't you ever come into my house calling my friend a liar, you disrespectful prick!" She had enough sense not to physically assault me in the apartment, she wanted to do it where no one was looking.

So that was that. I never ended up making friends with that group of guys. But as I got to know some other people around St. George that summer, the rumor at least partially died. All it takes is getting to know me, and people see the truth. I haven't changed Chris and Kaitlin's names, so I hope they see this. 😊 I guess the lesson of this story for me was: you can lead a neurotypical person to water, but you can't make them drink.

Every Story Is Bigger in Texas

Leaving Utah for Austin, Fall 2014

It was July of 2014 that my parents came out to see me for a weekend. I was beginning to feel guilty for my parents' spending money every month to pay for the program when I was pretty much doing everything on my own, and I let them know I felt it was time I graduated from ATC and Utah altogether.

In the back of my mind I had always known that I am meant to be an entertainer in some capacity, since making people laugh is the only thing I've always been better at than anybody else. Since Las Vegas is right next door to St. George, Utah, I figured it would be the most logical move to make, but my parents strongly disagreed. Out of the blue, my mom said, "How about Austin? I've heard great things about it—the weather is nice."

I had noticed that a disturbing number of kids that had gone through the program would end up just staying in St. George pretty much the rest of their lives—even though they didn't fit in at all to the family-oriented Latter-Day-Saints culture. In fact, they stuck out like a sore thumb. They just didn't have the will to pack up and relocate. I call that "letting life wash over you," and I was determined not to turn into one of those people. My real goal was to go to Los Angeles, but we all agreed that I wasn't ready. My parents and I agreed that Austin might be a good pre-L.A. place that would have some of the entertainment industry stuff I wanted to be involved in. There were a lot of comedy clubs with open mic opportunities several times a week. We decided that how I did in Austin, living on my own, would tell us if I could handle L.A.

My mom accompanied me to Austin to help me move into an apartment we found online. As soon as we got off the plane, I saw in the airport a giant sculpture of a hipster cowboy. Something about that one sight let me know what the city's character was like, and I thought, "What am I doing here? This isn't the right place for me."

As we explored the city, it quickly became clear that I was right about my initial gut feeling. You see, I had figured Austin was a big enough city that it wouldn't be one homogenous culture, but I was looking around at the whitest, most gentrified place I had ever witnessed in my life. This wasn't blonde-Republican-family-Utah-white—this was SWPL white (that stands for *Stuff White People Like*, the popular blog I mentioned earlier that satirizes urban, liberal white people—I'll be using this term a lot!) Austin was a hipster city full of white people that loved funky coffee shops, kayaking, and Subarus with "Coexist" bumper stickers. Even though I had moved beyond being totally into black culture, I knew I didn't fit in with SWPLs at all. I had absolutely nothing in common with them. However, my time in Austin ended up not being so bad, and I made the most of it. Welcome to the next chapter of my life.

Comedy Career or Get a Job?

I had moved to Austin in order to finally pursue my goal of being a comedian. YouTube hadn't quite blown up the way it is now, so I hadn't really thought of going the YouTube route. I was thinking of being a stand-up comedian. I had started doing stand-up when I was fifteen and felt I was pretty good at it. One of the big reasons I agreed to move to Austin was that I would be able to do open mic comedy every night. What I wasn't counting on was that, just like the rest of the city, the comedy scene was extremely specific to that same SWPL culture.

My first month there, I was going out on stage somewhere every night, trying out material. I got a notebook and started writing out all these bits, and really went for it. You would have never known it was a big city because it was the same small group of comedians at all the open mic nights. It would have been great had I fit into that culture, but I didn't make a single friend going out to these clubs. In fact, they were dicks to me, not nice people at all. The comedy aspect was a struggle too, which really set off an alarm for me. In my life full of inconsistency, the one consistent thing throughout, has been making people laugh. Whether it's at a dinner with my grandparents and friends or hanging out in jail, it's the only thing I have never struggled with! So if I was struggling to get laughs doing this comedy scene, something must be very wrong!

Austin is the second "city that never sleeps." You can go out every night of the week and find nightlife. It's very much a playground for adults. I must say, going from Utah to Austin was an enlightenment for me in terms of educating me on the flip side of white culture. If you're reading this and asking, "What is 'white culture?'" — go to Austin, my friend, you will see it.

In my new apartment there was a gay couple next door that I hung out with a few times. One of them had met me while I was moving boxes and immediately started flirting with me, so I tried to turn it into a friendship. I'm not sure if they were hanging out with me in the hope that I might be gay and do something, but I liked hanging out with them anyway.

Matt was white, and his partner, Carlos, was Hispanic. They were also new to Austin, and Carlos asked me what I thought of Austin.

I said, "It's a very white city."

He shot back, "I know, right!?"

White people often don't understand or recognize this. I guess it's like when you're a fish, you don't know you're in water. Meanwhile, Carlos knew exactly what I was talking about.

The culture of Austin made stand-up comedy DOA for me because that's absolutely not my audience. Just about everyone except SWPLs thinks I'm funny. So I stopped trying to do stand-up and decided to get a job.

I wanted to drive a taxi or maybe a limousine and found the perfect company. There were four or five people working there, and the husband and wife who owned it were really nice. However,

Austin has a ridiculous bureaucratic process to get a taxi license. This wasn't like Utah, where you take a thirty-five-question test for an endorsement to drive a commercial taxi. In Austin there was an Office of Transportation and they needed official state paperwork for every legal situation you have ever been in, stating the outcome of each case to prove that it was officially and legally closed. ☺

I'd had my share of legal issues by this point in my life, and in multiple states, so it was challenging to get that information. The owners of the taxi company were more patient about it than I was. They took me in and were great, helping me figure out the process and gather the things that I needed. My dad helped, too, getting all my court papers and mailing them to me.

As it turns out, the lawyer in Utah had never filed the final paperwork to close my case there, so that was another hurdle. I would go into the Office of Transportation, and they would tell me that I had a thirty-seven-dollar fine somewhere that looked like it hadn't been paid, so I would have to get all the paperwork to prove that it was. It was appalling to see where our tax dollars were going. They would find obscure things buried within all the paperwork of my life and say they needed more details.

A year later, after getting the final piece of paperwork they required, I went back to the same taxi company again. This would have been the perfect place for me to work. Again, they helped me out and, again, the city denied me the license. The woman I was dealing with was the kind of government employee that gives government employees a bad reputation. There will be a nice, warm hot tub for her in Hell.

When I finally got approved, I discovered that was just step one. The next step was a huge exam. It required mapping things out on an old-fashioned map, even though everyone uses a GPS. With my perilously low spatial IQ, this was exceedingly difficult, and there were no accommodations that could be made for my having a disability. It didn't go well.

So, until I found something better, I went back to work for Jimmy John's, the same sandwich shop chain I had worked for in

Utah. It was different in Austin because I was working in a downtown location. I had imagined a nightmare scenario when I first got my car in St. George: getting into an accident, wrecking my car, and losing my delivery job. As a joke in my head, I had thought, "What if I tried to go back to work and take deliveries on my bike? Can you imagine the horror?" I never imagined that job actually existed! But when I got to Austin, most of the delivery "drivers" at Jimmy John's were, in fact, on bikes! It made sense in Austin because, as I would come to find out, driving downtown sucked. There was tons of traffic, and you couldn't park anywhere, but the worst part was that driving was actually seen as uncool by the SWPLs. In St. George, literally the only people in the entire city riding around on bikes were guys from the ATC program. It was humiliating biking around a city where everybody drives. I had a couple of dates in St. George where I went out of my way to hide my bike because it was such a bad look. If I had had those same dates in Austin, I would have been able to show the bike off!

I kept the job with Jimmy John's for about three months. They were assh*les, and after almost forty jobs by age twenty-five, I don't say that about everyone I've worked for. I don't even say that about people who have fired me. But at the Austin Jimmy John's, they were assh*les. Granted, I did make my fair share of mistakes.

There was a strict policy that all the orders had to be taken in chronological order. Maybe there was the same policy at the other Jimmy John's I worked at, but it never became an issue. I took a couple of orders that someone else was supposed to take, so it looked like I was cherry-picking the orders. I got very defensive when confronted because I didn't realize what a big deal it was.

The manager was a guy I would describe as a caricature of a manager, like straight out of the movie *Office Space*. Except this guy was my age! He literally was like something out of a commercial where they portray a lame boss, trying to act all cool with his employees: "Dylan, whatchu doin' this weekend? Gonna party it up?"

Don't get me wrong, it wouldn't have been bad if he was a

nice guy, but underneath, he was genuinely a douchebag. There was another guy who was nice to everyone but me. Every time I asked him a question, he gave me an attitude like, "I can't believe you just asked me that question."

After about three months there, I went in one day and they pulled me aside and told me I had to take a pop quiz on all the sandwiches. No prepping, no studying, and no looking at the menu whatsoever. I had to face the window and write every single ingredient to every sandwich at Jimmy John's on a blank piece of paper.

Were they serious?

They had never told me that I had to memorize all the sandwiches, but I guess it's in the employee handbook that you must possess knowledge of the menu. I was given fifteen minutes to do the test. I only made it through half of the sandwiches because I wasn't prepared. (If you have read *Chasing the Rabbit,* you know that I'm in the one percentile for processing information.) I was genuinely trying, but they told me, "Sorry, your time's up."

Instead of telling me things weren't working out, or God forbid, telling me what I was doing wrong so I could improve it, they created an elaborate ruse to fire me, all in the name of avoiding awkwardness. The cowardice of most people never ceases to blow my mind. It ended up being a good thing because soon after that incident I got two jobs. I started working part-time for Edible Arrangements, which is one of the few jobs I never got fired from . . . because it was only seasonal. 😄 Working for Edible Arrangements was like seeing a girl who is only in town every couple of months. Since you don't see her very often, it's a lot less likely you'll screw things up or she'll get sick of you. I liked it because they paid me to drive all over the state of Texas in brand new rental cars, and it would be a different rental car every time! It was like a box of rental car chocolates. I started on Valentine's Day, and then I did Easter, and then for every holiday they kept calling me back. One day the boss told me I always showed up and got the deliveries done fast, and *that* was why she kept calling me to come back! That felt great! At the same time, I knew that was the kind of thing that could only happen at a seasonal job.

I loved the idea of getting paid to drive someone else's car, so I tried to get a valet job. It didn't work out once they saw my shop-lifting misdemeanor from Florida. However, in one of the inter-views I was telling the other guys applying that I wished I could find a delivery job where they let you drive their car. One guy said, "Dude, go to Sushi Zushi." I bet he didn't think I was going to remember that, but I did. As soon as I walked out of that interview I called Sushi Zushi to see if they were hiring. I went there, filled out the app, and I got a call a few days later that they wanted me to come in and start! That job ended up being the best thing that happened to me in Austin. The *Dirty Pop* thing that I will tell you about later was great too, but really the best thing in Austin was Sushi Zushi. It turned out to be almost the longest job I've ever held. (Jimmy John's in Utah was a little longer, at seven months.)

Sushi Zushi is an upscale sushi chain in Texas, and the job was to the T what I'd been looking for. Instead of using your own car, we were given Volkswagen Beetles to drive for deliveries. Turns out, VW bugs are super-fun cars to drive! I wouldn't be caught dead owning one, but since this was work, it was a perfect excuse to drive one!

Brent, the manager there, was hands down the best boss I have ever had. Even though it's usually an exercise in futility, I told them at Sushi Zushi about my disability. Something was different this time: Brent actually put things into action based on what I said.

I explained to them what I had come to observe about myself, that the way I learn best is not to have someone else do it for me. A lot of times, when people explain something to you, they show you what to do while you watch. When I watch someone else perform a task, I retain almost none of the information. I have to do it myself. Managers have to hold my feet to the flames, forcing me to figure it out without giving me the answer unless I really need it.

Sushi Zushi had a complicated computer system with a lot of items, and they didn't expect me to learn it right away. There were three hundred different kinds of sushi on the menu. (To me, all sushi tastes exactly the same, kind of like how all beer tastes the same—good, but the same.) They expected employees to gradually learn the sushi options, as well as the different kinds of rolls. One time I was standing there trying to remember some procedure with the software, it was like CTRL A + find something on the tab + hit ESC + right-click something or other, and I asked the assistant manager for help. I expected him to just jump on and do it for me because I'm so used to not actually being accommodated. Instead, he stood back and gave me one direction at a time, waiting for me to figure it out. I was taken aback—had advocating for my disability actually worked? It seemed too good to be true!

Turns out, it wasn't true for very long. Five months in, just when it looked like I might break my record, I got canned in August of 2015 for racking up three complaints about my driving. Like a rerun of Chili's, two of the complaints were my fault, and one wasn't. Once again, a three-strike corporate policy took me down. If you want the details of what happened check out the bonus chapters available on BadChoicesMakeGoodStories.com 😊

Chasing the Rabbit **Is Released**

My dad called me one day in January 2015. We mostly talk by texting, so when he calls me, it's usually serious. My mom sometimes calls me just to chat. Sometimes I feel like talking to her, and sometimes I don't. I know she likes it when we talk, so I try to keep her on the phone at least for a little while.

My dad rarely calls me and usually doesn't want to talk long. When he called me out of the blue, I wondered what it was all about.

"I wrote a book, and it's all about raising you," he said. "I want to publish it and share our story with people. I don't know if anyone will buy it, but I'll give you half the money if they do. After all, it's your story, too. What do you think?"

I think I shocked him when I came back with a quick, "Sure, I'm good with that." He was sure that I was going to say, "No way!

There's no way you're telling everyone my dirty laundry!" But I really was fine with it.

Then he said, "Who knows? We may even be able to do some speaking about it."

"I'd be great at that," I told him.

"Yeah, you probably would be," my dad said.

As of the writing of the book you're reading now, my dad and I have done a combined 101 presentations. Sometimes he presents alone, and I've done a few alone, but all of the big ones we've presented together.

We've appeared at conferences, schools, pretty much anywhere there's a stage. I never realized how natural public speaking would be for me and how much of an impact my story would have on people. Seeing people line up to meet me afterwards and take selfies with me was very cool. My dad texted my mom from a conference in Virginia, "Now I know how Ringo Starr felt." I told him he needed to update his references—'60s nostalgia is so '80s.

My dad always commits to the moment for photos

Becoming @RealDielawn, Winter 2015

As I did some self-reflection, I realized that with stand-up comedy, there's a heavy emphasis on punchlines; whereas the way I've always made people laugh is more like my sister once said, "his whole life is like a stand-up comedy act."

Funny ideas often seem to come out of my conversations with females, in trying to impress them. I had met a girl on Tinder my first week in Austin, and while we were watching TV I offered her some gum. Then I started bragging about how "I stay gummed out." I told her, "I got gum for days, whatever flavors you feenin' for, girl, I got the hookup . . ." Then, thinking out loud, I said, "What if I did a music video like that, like instead of a drug dealer, I'm a gum dealer . . ." She thought it was funny and said I should do it and throw sticks of gum at the camera. The idea was born.

I decided to turn my idea into a song parody, and I wanted to do Rick Ross's "Blowin' Money Fast," but that was an old song at that point, so I decided to make it a mashup of two songs. One of the biggest rap songs of 2014 was a joint called "Hot N***a" by Bobby Shmurda. Writing out the lyrics came easily, staying "Gummed Out" was my life. Ever since I quit smoking, you could never catch me riding without at least three packs on me.

I created an ad for someone to help me shoot the video. There were a lot of students in Austin, and I met up with a guy about my age in a café. I told Ben my plan for "Gummed Out." He really liked the idea, and he said, "I like you. I think you're a character. Let's make this happen."

I went to Costco and bought all kinds of gum in bulk. We did shots of me in Costco, showing off the gum. We did a shot in the mall, and we got some random girls in the food court to be in it. In the scene, I walk by and slide the gum onto the table like a drug dealer.

The biggest hurdle was finding a couple of black guys to be in the video. The beginning of the song was supposed to be two black guys confronting me in the hood. Despite its political correctness, Austin is actually very segregated, so I went to the black area, the east side. This was nothing like the music video-esque hoods of Fort Lauderdale—it was a run-down, neglected area of Austin, very depressing. Another depressing thing about Austin was that because of gentrification, most of the young African-American population had moved to Houston, leaving the east side looking like a black old folks' home.

I went to the H-E-B grocery parking lot and spent hours going up to every young black person I could find, handing out fliers to get someone to be in my video. I had to move around so they wouldn't kick me off the property. Finally, I found a black guy who said he had a friend that would do it with him. They were perfect for it! They were my age, looked fresh, and acted out the lines exactly as I pictured them. They didn't want much money for it even. I think I gave them each twenty-five dollars. Go watch it on YouTube and let me know how you think it came out! 😃 Just search "Gummed Out."

Pretty dope for a debut, right? At this point I started really stepping up the skits that I was doing. I tried to post one every couple of days, or I would make a meme. For example, I made a commercial where I said, "DON'T drink and drive, and DON'T text and drive—do BOTH at the same time!" To promote my "Gummed Out" video, I targeted young black audiences, and basically followed every black kid I could find on all my social media platforms. You have to give a little: you have to follow people and like their stuff so you can engage your audience. I was getting great feedback. I'm not used to things going perfectly and receiving unanimous approval from everyone, so it felt really special, like I was doing what I was meant to do. Even people that didn't like me or I'd had issues with in the past were sending me a few "😂😂"s. Sometimes the rawest truths come from those who don't like you. But the fact I had support from strangers too?! The experience affirmed what I had been hearing my whole life: I guess I'm funny.

I was very motivated, as soon as I had "Gummed Out" on my channel, to get another song parody vid together. Again, inspiration came from a conversation with a female. One night I was talking to a girl on the phone, and I told her how I want to make friends with gay guys but it's hard when you're not gay, and you just want to be friends! She said, "That should be your next song." Just like the guy in the valet interview who told me to check out Sushi Zushi, I bet she never expected two weeks later to see it up on YouTube.

Being a longtime Lady Gaga fan, I thought, what's more appropriate than to pick one of her songs to parody? I decided on doing her biggest hit, "Poker Face." My version was called "I'm Not Gay," and it ended up being my most successful video to date. If you want to see this one make sure you search YouTube for "I'm Not Gay Dielawn." (There are a lot of videos with that title!)

I titled my new video "I'm Not Gay" because it happened to match up lyrically with Lady Gaga's "Poker Face." I thought about doing her song "Born This Way," or maybe "Applause," but the part where she says "Poker Face" translated perfectly into "I'm Not Gay." It has the same number of syllables.

Most people got it, but there were a few that thought it was a song about people thinking I'm gay. This just offended me as a comedian. Did they really think I spent a good chunk of money, two weeks of running around, and hours on hours of editing to do a hacky concept that's been done to death? The song was about friendship. It was about yet another struggle that I had making friends. I had thought it was easy writing "Gummed Out," but writing this was even easier! It was absolutely the story of my life, and became even more so *after* it was posted on YouTube. 😂

Even more ridiculous were a few special people who thought I was actually *making fun* of gay stereotypes. One comment read, "Not all LGBT ppl are like that, God dame it"—to which I replied, "I'm like that, God dame it." All those "stereotypes" were true about me! And in almost every line of the song, I sing about wanting to make friends with gay people. One of the lyrics is, "I promise you, promise you, this could be a bad bromance"—a nod to Lady Gaga's other megahit, "Bad Romance." To try and call me homophobic was *really* a stretch.

To promote this video, I targeted Lady Gaga fans. You wouldn't believe how many Lady Gaga fans there are. When I say "fans," I mean true fanatics: people who have dedicated their entire social media to Lady Gaga fandom. Their user names are song references like gagashooker, thegirlunderyou, gypsymonster, and bornthisslay (you may not get these references, but any "Little Monster" would in a second). Many of these fans are not in the U.S. In Europe and South America, there is more of a cultural appreciation for pop music than we have here. Suddenly, people all over the world were watching my "I'm Not Gay" video. It was pretty wild!

Getting on the Radio: *Dirty Pop with Lance Bass*, Spring 2015

Around this time I was listening to a show on SiriusXM called *Dirty Pop Live with Lance Bass*. In case you don't know, Lance Bass was a member of the boy band *NSYNC. Lance is the one who came out as gay, and SiriusXM had a LGBT talk radio channel called OutQ that *Dirty Pop* was on. I tuned in one day out of boredom, and it was actually a really good show! Lance, his producer, and the writer for the show would talk about pop culture, TV, and music, and it was actually really intelligent commentary. One thing I hate is when talk radio shows neglect their audience, and it sounds like the hosts are just talking to each other, but on *Dirty Pop,* Lance and his crew were really good at keeping the audience engaged at all times. The more I listened, the more I thought, "Wow, how come nobody knows about this show?"

One day they were talking about how they wanted fans to do publicity stunts to promote the show. It sounded like nobody was stepping up to the plate, and I really wanted to let people know about this show!

One good thing about Austin is that it was full of artistic people who were eager to help. I found a woman with a nice camera who was willing to go out with me on a Saturday and do some hardcore shilling for *Dirty Pop*. I bought some poster board and made a colorful sign, as well as a plastic, cheerleader-looking thing that passed as a megaphone. Most importantly, on the show they called their fans "peanuts," so I went to Costco and loaded up on packages of peanuts to throw at people.

I yelled things like, "Tune in to *Dirty Pop Live with Lance Bass!* Your pop culture destination on your drive home from work!" and "Want some peanuts? They're honey-roasted!" (If you want to see this one, Google "Dielawn peanuts.")

When I submitted the video to the show, I didn't think much would come of it. I thought MAYBE they would retweet me or like it on social media. I turned on the radio the next day, and I heard my name! It was literally the second I turned on the radio: the first thing I heard was "Dielawn!" They couldn't stop talking about how creative my video was. They especially loved the throwing out peanuts bit. They said, "How did we not think of that?"

Have you ever watched VH1 *Behind The Music,* and the artists always talk about the first time they heard themselves on the radio? That's exactly what it was like, I was losing my mind! 😮

Later that night Drew, the *Dirty Pop* producer, found me on Facebook and messaged me. He told me he knew I wasn't an actual listener because their audience consisted of middle-aged women who have stalked Lance since his *NSYNC days, but he said, "I don't give a sh*t, we still want to work with you." I told him I actually listened to the show every day! As we know, I have Asperger's, and I can only do things well when I'm really interested in them. This wasn't me picking a random show and sucking up to the people on it for the fame. *Dirty Pop* and doing music videos were basically my special interest at this time. Also as we know, when I have a special interest, I'm all in. I give it a hundred percent, and I usually become a master. What made my video great was that I really believed what I was saying. Drew went on to tell me they have a lot of fans who submit things to the show, but it's usually some bad photoshopped graphic that they tweet out to fifty followers. In contrast, I was "this young, energetic, talented guy," and he was really excited to see what I could do.

From there, I quickly became a regular on the show. I started creating and editing segments where I would interview people on the street. Since I was stuck in the SWPL capital, I thought, "Why not create a segment based on the *Stuff White People Like* blog?" I took a recording mic around Austin and asked white people if they really liked random things like getting drunk and floating down a river, or Bill Nye the Science Guy. Turns out, they do! Then for my next segment, I went out and interviewed non-white people to see how they felt about the white people stuff. An Indian guy had never heard of Bill Nye, and a black guy told me, "I'm always floatin', but I ain't on a river, doe."

They would dedicate an entire hour of the show to making a game out of my segments, playing my questions and then pausing to guess what the people were going to say. Then the producer would have me call in, and they would basically shower me in praise for ten minutes. After two months at it, my content was being broadcast on a national gay talk radio station, by a former boy band member. You couldn't have cooked up in a lab a more perfect scenario of catching every rabbit I was chasing at that time. I had gone from wanting to make gay friends to making celebrity gay friends! But I wanted to take it to the next level and really make something out of this. I had an idea brewing in my head: I would make a music video that would be a parody of the song "Pop" (the *NSYNC song the show was named after) and write it as a commercial for the show!

Once again, I printed fliers looking for backup dancers, and it gave me a great excuse to go hang out at gay clubs! The process of getting the video together over the next couple of months was a grind, but when it finally came together it was another one of those rare times in life where something actually materializes exactly as I had imagined. Go see if it's everything you imagined in your head—YouTube "Dielawn Dirty Pop."

What did you think? My favorite parts were 2:33 and, obviously, 1:57. As soon as the video dropped, Lance invited me to L.A. to be a guest on the show. Oh, and the best part was: they did the show from a studio at his house! Are you kidding me?! My first trip to Los Angeles, I would be a guest on a national radio show hosted by Lance Bass—*at his house?!* I wish I could have gone back in time and told my ten-year-old self that this would happen, although 2001 Dylan would have probably told 2015 Dylan, "You're a liar, and I'm a Backstreet Boys fan."

I showed up at Lance's house, and his female assistant greeted me at the door. I asked her if this was Lance's house, and she said, "Yes, are you Dielawn?" That was very cool! Now, I will admit I downed a whole strawberry lemonade Four Loko before I got there. You might be expecting me to say, ". . . and I regretted my decision"—but no, thank God I did, because it went perfectly. 😁 Thanks, Four Loko!

I sat in for the whole show as an in-studio guest. After the show they always took group photos with the guests for Instagram, so we did that, and then I made sure to get one of just Lance and me. When I was leaving, I had Drew send me the pictures—I was so nervous I wasn't going to like how I looked, but they were perfect! Fun fact: they posted our group photo on their Instagram, and the day before I was there, their guest was '80s' pop star Taylor Dayne, so my photo is right next to hers. 😁

We live in a world of pics or it didn't happen, so the photo mattered as much as the actual interview. For months I had been bragging to everybody I knew about being featured on Lance Bass's show. Perception is reality—now that I had a photo, it was real. 100

Staying a regular presence on the show for as long as I did was all about keeping their attention, so I didn't waste any time pitching them my next idea. I said to Lance, "Did you know that *NSYNC had two Top 20 hits on Urban Radio?"

"I did not know that," he said.

I went on to tell them that I was a pop music encyclopedia and quickly pitched a new weekly segment called "Music News with Dielawn." I told them I could count down the top songs on Top 40 radio that week, and then I would write a couple of features, like

"Hit songs rejected by other artists" or "Two-hit wonders." They went for it, and they also added a piece at the end called "Deep Dive with Dielawn," where Lance would ask me questions to try and stump me. They basically had me writing the entire script for the segment—let me tell you, it was pretty insane sitting in my room typing out words that Lance Bass was going to read on the radio the next day. Sometimes they would be replaying Thursday's show and I would be in the car and just turn on the radio and hear myself. I was on top of the world! But this is my life we're talking about, so guess what happened: after moving the show to Andy Cohen's channel, RadioAndy, SiriusXM cancelled *Dirty Pop with Lance Bass*, along with the entire OutQ channel. *Dirty Pop* went out with a bang though, opening the last show by playing my song! ☺

Seeing my name on SiriusXM was pretty surreal!

Ridin' with Dielawn, 2016

The timing of the *Dirty Pop* cancellation worked out okay, because I had started a weekly radio show in Portland, Maine, on 100.5 FM WLOB called *Ridin' with Dielawn.* I was still in Texas, so I was doing it remotely and sending it to the station. The hour long show took more time than I thought it would. My initial idea was a spin-off of my "Music News with Dielawn" segments on Lance's show.

On my first show, I did a countdown of the Top 10 ten songs of the week. Then, in the second part of the show, I did a segment exploring why Sweden is a powerhouse of pop and electronic dance music.

Sweden is the largest exporter of pop music per capita in the world. The man responsible for you-wouldn't-believe-how-many songs you've heard over the last twenty years (in fact, as I'm writing this, he's written or produced sixty-seven *Billboard* Top 10 hits) is Sweden's Max Martin. Sweden is a socialist country, and there are lots of music and arts programs funded by the government. It's also dark half the year, so people stay inside and master the synthesizer.

A short time after I started *Ridin' with Dielawn,* I turned on the TV and everything was about the presidential race and how insane it was getting. I never thought I would be interested in politics, but I think a lot of people thought that prior to 2016. Politics suddenly became pop culture, so it was the perfect time for me to get interested in it.

I started covering the debates. It's kind of embarrassing, but for a second there I thought Bernie Sanders was going to be the next president, and I made that bold prediction on the air. It looked to me like the same thing that had happened with Barack Obama and Hillary Clinton was about to happen again, and I thought I was being really clever. It was funny because people interpreted my prediction as meaning I supported Bernie Sanders. But I didn't say that, I said I *thought he was going to be the next president.* Where in that statement did it say I *wanted* him to be the next president? I found this to be an interesting juxtaposition of my autistic, logical interpretation of the statement versus neurotypical people's emotional interpretation of my statement. Usually someone who makes an assertion like that would do it because they're rooting for that candidate; I said it because I thought it was true. And I found it to be really obtuse that people assumed emotions instead of listening to my words. Of course, I ended up being wrong, so I hope no one remembers. 😏

I finished the show with a segment I called "Dating with Dielawn." I did a rant talking about how sex is like coffee. My analogy: "I don't always really want coffee until I'm about to have coffee. And as soon as I finish the coffee, it's like, "Why did I want coffee?" It takes a lot of work to make it, and you end up with empty wrappers and a mess all over the counter afterwards."

I would continue with the radio show through the end of 2016, and you'll learn why soon.

Everything I Want, Right Before I Leave: Spring 2016

In the spring of 2016, I had gotten a summer job in Maine as a counselor at a camp for kids with disabilities. I largely viewed moving to Austin as a misstep due to my not fitting in with the SWPLs there, and I felt like it had mostly been a waste of time. I was happy to use my summer gig as an excuse to leave.

Knowing my time in Texas was limited, I started partying really hard. Edible Arrangements was calling me in more and more to fill in when they needed help. I would work a couple of days here and there and make some good money from that. I continued recording my weekly radio show but otherwise I pretty much had no responsibilities.

I know I seem like I have an answer for everything, but there is at least one recurring phenomenon in my life that has me completely at a loss. It always seems like right before I leave somewhere, the best thing there happens. In other words, I meet the people I have wanted to meet the whole time I was there. Either I will suddenly make a great new group of friends or a girl comes into my life out of nowhere, but it's always right as I am about to leave forever. It's frustratingly tragic. You could say it's like how Britney Spears had more number one hits than in her entire career only just before she got too old to get played on the radio anymore.

Perhaps the saddest example of this is the most recent-to-date. As mentioned, my time in Austin was when I was really trying to fit in with gay guys. I had made a few friends (and gotten on a national gay radio show), but I wanted to be that straight guy that hangs out with all the coolest gay guys. I wanted everyone at the gay clubs to know my name, and I wanted to be invited to the coolest after-parties. And I got everything I wanted, but only less than two months from when I would be leaving for good.

I went out on a Sunday afternoon in April 2016. The clubs in Austin are open in the daytime on weekends, and many go there to drink and talk. I find it much nicer to be at a club in the daytime, when it's more laid back than it is at night. I met a guy named Noah, who introduced me to his friends, and we started hanging out. I was starting to get into politics and was really fascinated by the presidential election. One of the guys Noah introduced me to was Jeff Simpson, a gay Republican journalist and commentator. He was president of the Houston Republicans Club or something like that. Jeff and his friend had a hotel room they were partying at, and we went over there and hung out till 6:00 a.m. the next morning.

As social dynamics go, oftentimes all it takes is meeting that one right person, and it's a snowball effect. They bring you around their friends, who in turn introduce you to their friends, and all of a sudden your social life blows up. So my wish came true: I was in the club one night in May 2016 and I heard my name called from every direction; there were three different groups of people that wanted me to hang with them. I had been partying all the time, but there was something different this time—it was with people I could actually trust. I was making friends with intelligent, professional, high-quality people who weren't going to rob me if I passed out or take my car without permission or any of the other things people have done to me.

Brunch Mimosas with the gays in Austin!

I had tried all the typical party drugs: molly, cocaine, ecstasy pills. I think because of the autism, and how intensely logical my mind is, I noticed it would take a lot more drugs to get me to feel something than other people. I would spend half the night in my head like, "Wait, am I high?" "Is the drug working?" One of the drugs popular in Texas is, of course, crystal meth. Logically thinking, meth is a stronger version of coke, so I said to myself, "Why not give it a try? Maybe I'll actually feel it!" You might be horrified at this, but when you're partying in Texas, you wouldn't believe how many seemingly normal people do this stuff. Being very susceptible to external influences, when I saw how ubiqui-tous meth was, it was normalized for me into just another party drug. However, unlike the other party drugs, I definitely knew I felt something. Finally, I had found a drug where I didn't sit there all night questioning if I was high! This was the real deal—this was freakin' meth! 😲

You may be thinking that it's bizarre I thought so highly of these new friends because they were doing drugs with me. How could they be quality people? Again, Austin is a playground for adults; if there is any city where you're going to find good people with bad habits, it's Austin, Texas.

One friend I really wish I had met sooner was a guy named Dave. I had a few friends over one night that I'd met out clubbing, and they invited him over. I walked into my kitchen and saw a Drake lookalike standing at my counter. I said to him, "You look like you're black and Jewish."

"I am!" he said, and a friendship was made. Yet again, Dave proved that I indeed have the musical taste of a gay black guy—he knew even the most obscure pop songs that I loved (like Anjulie, "Brand New B*tch").

I ended up having more fun those last two months in Austin than I had the entire time I had been there added up. I was doing meth pretty much every day. I was also doing something called GHB, or "G," which is technically a date rape drug, but as long as you don't get date raped, it's really fun. In fact, it was literally the best thing I had ever tried. Putting meth and G together was one hell of a ride. This probably sounds ridiculous, but it felt like God was giving me this awesome time to be young and live it up, so I did.

As I have said, the pattern of my whole life is that nothing good lasts long. My good times in Austin were coming to an end.

My Thoughts on God

During the book tour for *Chasing the Rabbit*, I spent a lot of time with my dad. He likes to ask me serious questions at dinner. I think he does it to try to understand me better and to avoid sitting in silence while I'm on my phone. One night in Denver, I started the conversation. Out of the blue I said, "If there's a God, he must hate me."

My dad was surprised by the sudden, harsh statement. "Why would you say that?" he asked.

I said, "Because nothing ever goes well for me for long. My life always goes back to being garbage at some point."

He tried to convince me that God does love me, because of all the times my life could have become a disaster but came just short of it. I wasn't convinced, but he made some good points.

I would like to believe there is a God, and I always tried to when I was a kid, but the problem is that my brain only thinks in logical terms. There is nothing logical about God. And the rhetoric in church all just sounds so esoteric to me. The emotional and spiritual concepts described in religious services seem to connect with neurotypical people on some deep level, but I just don't have that level.

My dad said, "Well, try praying. Just ask God for guidance and see if you hear anything in your head."

That sounded very nice, but I explained to him the problem with that plan, "If I listen to God and try to hear what I think God is telling me to do, but it's just my own thoughts—and then, because I always make bad decisions, it doesn't work out well—I'll be mad at God. Right now, I'm not feeling anything toward God, good or bad, which is better than being mad at God."

My dad tried to change my thoughts on that by saying, "Dylan, if you think you hear God giving you advice, and then it doesn't work out, it was you. God would never lead you down a bad path."

The issue I often run into when people try to give me advice is that I am very good at covering my bases, so people's suggestions are either things I've already tried or ideas I've already thoroughly thought through. This leads me to say things like, "Well I did that and X happened" or "The problem with that is X" and then the other person feels like I'm arguing with them instead of taking their advice. *Sigh* 😐

I told my dad, every time I have tried to include God in my daily thoughts, it has led to a feedback loop of what feels like insanity because I cannot differentiate between my own thoughts and what "God" might be telling me. I end up going crazy and it turns me off to the whole thing, so why not just leave it alone? Fingers crossed I won't go to hell!

Dirty Pop at Sea, April 2016

So *Dirty Pop Live* had been abruptly cancelled, but it wasn't over quite yet. I didn't know this was a thing, but there had been a Caribbean cruise planned for fans of the show. "Dirty Pop at Sea" was still happening, but tickets were a thousand dollars, so I had figured I wouldn't be making that. Then, out of nowhere, two women who were fans of the show and of my segments offered to pay for my ticket! It got even better because there was a super-cool gay guy known on the show as "Dustin From Seattle" who would always call in and talk about me. I was going to be rooming with him on the ship! I thought this would be an awesome time—why would I think otherwise?

I met up with Dustin at the port in Ft. Lauderdale, and he had a female friend with him. She was a thirty-something, very overweight woman who was cold and unfriendly to me. I assume she was a little jealous because she was supposed to be there as Dustin's friend. I was thinking, "Lady, you live near him, you get to see him all the time. I only have this week!" I hate how people never seem to take that into consideration.

When we finally got through all the paperwork, we got on the ship. This cruise ship was actually the biggest one in the world, not even kidding. (I heard that every year they make a bigger one, but that year, it was this one.) So naturally I was expecting a modern day *Titanic*. I was expecting grand staircases and big-ass chandeliers. But it felt more like a 3-star hotel; like a DoubleTree by the airport.

There was a "meet and greet" for our group in a conference area where we got to take pictures with Lance and his husband, Michael Turchin. They both recognized me, which felt good!

Then I met the women who paid for my ticket. Tammy and Lynn were a lesbian couple in their thirties from Georgia who were actually getting married on the cruise, and Lance was reading their vows. It was the most bizarre thing, because they weren't at all friendly—they barely said hello to me, *even though they had spent a thousand dollars to put me on this cruise with them!* I tried to tell them how grateful I was and congratulate them on their marriage, but they hardly wanted to speak with me. I realized later it may not have been because of me.

Our group was about fifty people, and now I saw exactly what Drew had told me when we met: it was almost entirely middle-aged women, a couple husbands that had been dragged along, and I was literally the only single straight guy there. I was expecting that to be the case, but I thought they would at least like me. I tried to be nice and friendly to everyone, as I always do, but there was a palpable unwelcoming feel—a feminized atmosphere that reminded me of when I worked at T.J. Maxx and other retail stores where the staff gave off a cliquey, middle-school-ish "You're-not-getting-invited-to-the-lunch-table" vibe. I thought people would be excited to meet me from hearing me on the show every week, but it turned out most of the women were just there for Lance and didn't even listen to the show! I liked Lance, but I *loved* his show—that's what I was there for. I mean, it was called "Dirty Pop at Sea" . . .

It would have been a lot cooler if Andy, the show's writer (the other straight guy), and Drew, the producer, had been able to make it, because they had really been my biggest fans through the whole thing. Dustin, however, was just as cool as I thought he would be, and he told me he was also disappointed about how socially awkward and lame all the women were. I thought maybe I wasn't crazy after all!

Outside of our little group, the rest of the cruise was just as disappointing. I wasn't just the only straight, single, young person in our group; I might have been the only straight, single, young person on the whole cruise! There were zero hot girls. It looked like the early bird special at Old Country Buffet: nothing but frumpy families with little kids and older married couples. I did *not* expect that! I figured, "Caribbean cruise"—I thought this would be like a party!

If you have ever been to a nightclub, you know the staff largely turns a blind eye to the drug use that goes on. I honestly thought the cruise would be a lot like a gay nightclub or even a gay after-party at someone's apartment in downtown Austin. I figured Dustin did drugs because he seemed like the party type. But when I got to the cruise he told me he didn't. He said he had grown up with his whole family abusing drugs, so he had never touched them, and that I should just stick to the drinks.

I was smart enough not to bring any drugs with me. But I wanted to try to buy some on one of the Caribbean islands we stopped at during the cruise. I wanted to leave the tourist area and go find the hood!

Our first stop was in the Virgin Islands. As soon as we got off I walked until I didn't see any more white people in sight. I was literally in the ghetto of the Virgin Islands, I was pretty excited. I used the same principles as when I would go through the hood in Florida: act confident, act like you belong there. I went up to a couple of young black guys and quietly asked them if I could buy some "yayo" (cocaine). I knew there was a strong chance they would think I was a cop, but I asked anyway. Then a Hispanic guy approached me in a very friendly manner and asked, "What's up man, you need help with anything?" If you have ever been to a third world country you know exactly what I'm talking about. He was very nice and very helpful, and he ended up taking me for a ride around town in his car, a beat-up hatchback from the '80s that I couldn't believe was running. He took me to buy two bags of cocaine for thirty bucks, and I gave him a nice tip.

I had never bought drugs by myself before, and the fact that I had just made a real life drug deal happen, without getting ripped off—*in the hood of the Virgin Islands*—was another one of those moments for me that was as exciting as making those black guys in jail laugh. I wanted so badly to post a video on Snapchat telling everyone what I had just done, but I stopped myself. It may sound degenerate, and you can judge me all you want. But you have to remember: even though I was twenty-four at this time, my maturity level was probably like a seventeen- or eighteen-year-old, and this was a big deal for me. I was *so* proud of myself.

I don't understand going to a foreign place and just sticking to the tourist spots. It doesn't make sense to me. I feel the same way about so-called "sightseeing." For me, real sightseeing includes seeing the places tourists don't go, seeing the actual culture, and how people are living. It disturbs me that I'm in the minority when it comes to thinking like this! When I was in middle school, my grandparents took my sister Mariah and me to Europe. We visited Paris and London. I drove them all crazy as I tried to become as much a part of the actual culture as possible, including asking a French girl if I could get a French kiss, and getting chased out of a red light district for taking photos of a sex shop.

Looking back now, I feel like the fact that the actual cruise went so poorly, might have been God telling me something like "this is what happens when you do drugs." Over the past year, every bit of involvement I'd had with *Dirty Pop* had been like a dream come true. It had just been homerun after homerun. Unfortunately, since the cancellation in February, I had started going out a lot and really going to town with drugs.

By the fifth day of the cruise, I became so uncomfortable by these two women (the ones who paid for my ticket!) continuously coming around and being super friendly to everyone but me, that I actually had to ask Dustin to say something. After he did, they suddenly started acting super nice towards me. However, if I hadn't brought drugs into the equation, I just feel like the whole cruise would have gone better. It seemed so bizarre that there was no other way to explain it than a higher power intervening and giving me a sign.

Don't G and Drive

The thing about meth is that it magnifies whatever is most important to you. Luckily I have never had to witness this but I have heard that for many people, it's sex. That's not the case for me. For me, the most important thing above anything else is always going to be, you guessed it—pop music. The best thing about doing meth with gay friends was that they liked to talk about pop music! I would bring people over and just play music videos all night.

Between the friends, the pop music and the meth, life was good. But the first time I realized the drugs were becoming problematic for me was one night when I was up all night doing GHB and lines of meth with my friends Rob and Justin. I was having a blast. Having autism, and my life being a long series of mistake after mistake, I always have to try so hard not to screw up. Being on meth truly made me not care what was going on: I could finally chill out and enjoy the moment. I wondered: is this what it's like to be a neurotypical person all the time? Is this what it's like even *some* of the time? It felt like I was in the sky, like a true party in my brain. It was the same thing every time, but it never got old.

So there we were, hanging out, blasting music videos off YouTube. I always joked that the more f*cked up I got, the more my taste in music regressed. I would start off the night with a top song currently on the radio, and by 5 a.m. I would be playing songs I used to sing when I was six. Ironically, we were listening to the Spice Girls song "Stop" when I got a call from Edible Arrangements. I had just taken another dose of G and was at the top of my high, and I had completely forgotten telling them that I could come in that day. I was already late when they called me; I'd gotten another missed call and a text!

As high as I was, the second I saw "Edible Arrangements" pop up on my phone, I felt my heart sink. I knew I might have screwed up enough to lose the job and I didn't know what to do! I spent half an hour deliberating whether to go in or not, making me even later for work. I knew I had to, or they would never call me again.

I was hours away from being in any shape to drive, though. I started getting frantic and asked my friends: if I paid them fifty dollars, would they meet me in the parking lot, and then drive the Edible Arrangements car for me for a few hours, so I could just sit in the passenger seat and go make the deliveries? Of course this was way against company policy, but honestly, it was probably less against company policy than me driving on meth and G.

If you think driving drunk is bad, let me tell you: driving on G is infinitely worse. GHB messes with your equilibrium so you can't even stand up straight. Normally when you're in a car you'll feel it as it's turning, but when you're on G you can't even steer it.

No one was down to that scheme with me because they didn't know me that well. Rob was actually a big time meth dealer, he was a really masculine gay guy whom you would never know was gay. I had been to Rob and his partner's house, and they were basically white-collar, professional drug dealers. They had a toolbox containing every kind of drug you could possibly imagine, each drug labeled and categorized. They had Excel spreadsheets and a computer database of their clients. He could talk your ear off about all the scientific details of making meth, the chemical composition, and the physics of this bong versus that bong.

I asked Rob if he could at least drive me into work, about twenty minutes away, so I would have some time to come down off my G high. I arrived at Edible Arrangements and gave the acting performance of my life! I was still rolling on G and could barely walk straight. Yet, I somehow summoned up the will to walk into Edible Arrangements, look my boss straight in the eye and talk to her as if I was perfectly fine.

Driving that car out of the lot was one of the scariest things I have ever done. Not only could I barely even feel the car, but it was also raining. I got thirty seconds down the road before I had to pull over. I just sat there and listened to some Fifth Harmony on full blast until I felt somewhat down from the high. Even though I miraculously got every customer their chocolate-covered pineapples that day, I was starting to sense that I had to get control of my drug use. I have been fired almost forty times! This was one of the few jobs I had not only kept, but my boss had *just* got done telling me how great I was the last time I saw her! And now this. I felt genuinely a little bad, like I had betrayed the only place that liked me. But what would come later as a result of my drug use made this incident look charming.

Girl Problems in Texas, Fall 2015

In August 2015 I met Caroline. She was a super cute, half-Mexican, half-Italian girl with a bangin' body and a sweet personality. She stuck out to me on Tinder because she wrote in her bio that she was obsessed with Justin Timberlake. I figured, that meant she liked white guys who dress fresh—I was just her type. Plus hello—who else was she going to meet closer to Justin Timberlake than the guy on Lance Bass's radio show?

We ended up dating for a few months. Being with her made me over-the-moon happy, and I really wanted it to work out. It was approaching Thanksgiving, and I asked my mom if Caroline could come with me this year. I won't pretend it wasn't partly because I wanted to show her off to my whole family—I definitely did.

My mom said, "I don't know, Dylan—that's a big step. It might be a little intimidating for a new girlfriend. Doesn't she want to be with her own family at Thanksgiving?"

I said, "Mom, you really think I'm dating someone with a good family life? I never date girls with fathers!"

She was taken aback and said, "What do you mean?"

I hit her with a different perspective on the world, as I often do. "I love girls with no fathers!" I said. "Think about it. Any girl with a strong father figure in her life is going to be looking for a man who's like her dad. And I'm not going to be like anyone's dad! My only chance at a long-term relationship is with a girl who doesn't have a good father to compare me to."

My mom was speechless. She thought it was very sad, but she could see the logic behind it. She was impressed with how deeply I had thought about the issue. As I wrote earlier when talking about the "normal" theory at Northeastern University, I have many profound thoughts every day. On this day I shared one with my mom.

Caroline and I, however, never made it to Thanksgiving. It ended really badly, for me anyway. She lied to me, telling me she wasn't in the right frame of mind to be in a relationship. And then, sure enough, a couple of weeks later I saw her on Snapchat clearly with another guy, who was way uglier than me (that was the most offensive part).

Keep in mind, I had done okay for myself, but dating Caroline for three months was one of the first legitimate relationships I had ever had, and losing her was one of the most painful things I've ever been through. It was like the pain when a girl I've only been out with once stops responding, times a thousand. I couldn't think about anything else for weeks; it was like a physical pain right in my stomach. I wondered why my breakup with Mandy back in Florida hadn't been as painful, even though she was very special. I realized it was because we didn't have sex. The fact that Caroline and I had been so intimate made the pain of her walking away so much deeper. Now I understood why they told me in church youth group that you should save sex for marriage. But it was something I needed to experience, because it gave me a new perspective on relationships. That was the parting gift her lies gave me: I finally overcame the feeling that I was incomplete without a girlfriend.

My thinking was always: "If I could just get a girlfriend, then I wouldn't have to be single anymore, and everything would be great." But I found that once you get a girlfriend, the game never stops. There's the constant fear of, "What if I screw this up?" And the more time goes by, the more invested you become, and the more you'll be hurt if she walks away. Avril Lavigne once put it: "Held up so high, on such a breakable thread." (Can you name the song? No Googling! 😊)

I realized that what had happened with Caroline would be an inevitable pattern in any relationship I have:

1. Girl likes me, I like the girl.
2. We get together.
3. I think, "Wow, this is great!"
4. I quickly care way too much.
5. I do a terrible job hiding it.
6. She gets turned off, and I lose her.

As much as I can try and have a positive outlook on it, I know myself. There is just no way I can have a girlfriend and act like I don't care. I'm just not that guy. Based on my dad's personality, I think I would have a hard time anyway, but then the autism adds an extra inability to conceal my emotions. If I care about her, she's going to know it!

I know you might be reading this, baffled by what I'm saying. Are you thinking, "You sound like a perfect boyfriend! What's wrong with caring?" Well, keep in mind that most relationships are not that serious. People tend to assume whenever you bring up any kind of relationship, that it's some kind of long-term commitment you're talking about. When you're just dating, caring is a recipe for disaster—unless maybe you're fifty and on eHarmony.com. You don't ever really *have* a girl—it's more like *renting* a girl. For females, the game *truly* never stops. They don't stop getting hit on just because they're in a relationship. Whereas us guys, (at least me, anyway) tend to take it seriously and just check out of the game. Even if the girl isn't hitting on the guys back, the point is she's interacting with potential suitors on a constant basis. So, if she walks away, she has about twenty different prospects waiting in the wings, meanwhile because I took the relationship seriously, I'm left with nothing. To girls in their twenties, men are utterly disposable. Feel free to send your daughter to prove me wrong. 😉

I would be lying if I said that when I hang out with a girl I'm not always thinking about turning it into a relationship, but I'm generally at peace with being single now. When I used to see other couples making out or holding hands in public, it used to drive a knife through me. Now that I've been to the other side, I understand that the grass isn't greener.

Caroline and me, seeing this after the breakup sucked.

If Edible Arrangements Were a Girl: Krissy

Of course, the best way to get over someone, is meeting someone new. When I was finally ready to re-download Tinder, I met a chica by the name of Krissy. She looked like the type of girl that usually goes for me. She had a *Jersey Shore* thing going on with big done-up hair, a lot of makeup, and pictures at EDM (electronic dance music) festivals. The best thing about her, though—she also loved cats! Usually when a girl loves cats, it's a good sign for me.

Now, Krissy wasn't quite as hot as Caroline, but now that I had been with a really hot girl and had seen the enormous amount of work it took, I was tired of my own standards. Krissy lived in the Dallas area, though, and only came down to Austin occasionally to visit family. Ironically, knowing right from the start that it couldn't be a full-time relationship let me relax and just enjoy my time with her.

One Friday night in December 2015 we met up and hung out for the night. It turned out we had a lot more in common than just cats, she also loved to turn up on Four Lokos, my all-time favorite drink. Four Lokos used to be the sh*t when I lived in Florida, but nowadays it's rare to find someone else who admits to liking them. She also liked to do X pills, which I had been messing around with at the time, so we got along pretty well. Her personality was intense, very bubbly and flirty—she would always be like, "What are you thinking?" Honestly, I thought she was a little much when I was with her, but the next day I couldn't get her out of my head. As soon as that overbearing, very girly personality of hers was gone, I really missed it.

I think it's a myth that men don't care what's in a girl's head. I think it's a stereotype that's used to dehumanize men. I've met a lot of girls whose personalities have ruined their looks in my eyes. And I've met girls whose personalities made me attracted to them. If a girl can make me laugh, that's a turn-on. If she's sassy and sarcastic, that's really hot. Those characteristics can be just as important as looks.

A couple of weeks later Krissy actually drove four hours to come see me in Austin and do it all over again. We got some Four Lokos and popped some more X pills. It was the holiday season, and the next day they called me in to work for Edible Arrangements. Driving around delivering chocolate-covered fruit on a balmy Christmas Eve, once again, all I could think about was Krissy.

I didn't see her for a little while, but then in March she messaged me and wanted to know what I was doing for South by Southwest (SXSW), a huge annual music festival in Austin. I was like, "You tryin' to have a lil reunion?"—and she said, "Yesss."

Colton was a friend of mine from ATC who lived in Texas, and he was in town for SXSW, too. He and I went over to meet up with Krissy and her sisters at their hotel. This was exciting, I love introducing new friends to old friends!

It had been a couple of months, and my first thought when I saw Krissy again was that she looked hotter than last time. When we got to the hotel room and met her sisters, they struck me as the polar opposite of her. They were monsters, and I don't mean Lady Gaga fans. They were each probably two hundred pounds heavier than Krissy, and they were viciously mean to her. They were very nasty and unhappy people in general. Meanwhile, Krissy was such a kind and sweet person that I couldn't understand how she could be related to these vile women.

Of course, I think a big part of it might have been that I was obviously a guy they could never get, and I was being invited up to their hotel room by their much hotter little sister. I could feel the jealousy in the room, and it made me feel pretty damn special. 😀

Suddenly, Krissy had to get something from her car, and Colton and I were left alone with her crazy sisters. As soon as she left the room, I felt the need to fill the silence. I blurted out, "I really like your sister. I don't know what it is about her, but every time I'm with her, the next day I can't stop thinking about her."

They seemed to let their guard down for a second, "Oh my God, that is so sweet!" they said.

As soon as Krissy came back to the room, one of her sisters discovered she had lost a twenty-dollar bill, and they both started screaming at Krissy and blaming her for the missing money. Pretty soon they were all screaming at each other and throwing things around the room! It was like a live scene from *Maury* or *The Jerry Springer Show* and, truthfully, I was on cloud nine.

The great thing about watching a fight is that you don't have to hide how entertained you are because the people in the fight are so caught up in the moment that they don't care about you being a spectator. As I sat there in heaven with my jaw dropped, I looked over at Colton, and he had a look of excruciating pain on his face. Not everyone lives for the drama like I do. If there's a link between that and autism, it probaby has to do with me generally not being on the same emotional wavelength as other people. It might be that disconnect that enables me to objectively enjoy an argument like it's entertainment.

Eventually things calmed down, and we went out and walked around downtown. The weekend was great. It was nice to see Krissy again and it felt like our "relationship" was becoming something—I wasn't sure what, but something. Everything with her was so effortless, I kept thinking, "So this is what it's supposed to feel like."

The next night we had a lot of adventures. They say it's good if you can bring a girl to multiple places rather than just bringing her home because it builds rapport and trust.

Remember that I talked about how I like bad girls who like to party? That might have been partly what attracted me to Krissy. She was twenty, which is usually the age people mess around with drugs. I was twenty-four, and I was going through the same phase in my life, so I felt like we were walking a similar path.

I introduced her to another friend that weekend, one of my gay black friends, Tay. Tay was a drag queen who came into my car with a group of people once and asked if he could connect his phone to play a song, which is usually an eye-roller, like, "Okay fine," right? Then the song he played was Janet Jackson's "Feedback," and I said, "That was the next song I was gonna play anyway!"

Tay did meth and was always very generous about sharing it. I remember the first time I told Krissy that I had done meth. I laughed as I said, "You'll never guess what I did last night. Me and my friends did some lines of meth!" She acted surprised and said "Hahaha, wtf?" She told me she didn't do that. As I sat there cutting up some lines on a plate in my car, Krissy all of a sudden said, "Here, give me that." She whipped out a card from her wallet and started going to town like a professional. I said "Wow, you *have* done this before!"

We did a few lines and got superman high. When I was on meth, it was like I wasn't really in the moment, I was detached from everything, and I didn't care about anything that was happening around me. Nothing around me mattered. But yet I was also enjoying the moment in a way I never could sober.

I don't know what you're thinking about me as you read this, but you need to understand how good that felt to me. If you have read *Chasing the Rabbit,* or even if you've made it this far in this book, you realize that my life has been tumultuous. I've spent much of my life extremely frustrated and anxious because I am forever chasing a rabbit that is just out of my reach. Can you imagine what that would be like? So, can you imagine how freeing it would be to suddenly not give a flying f*ck about any of that? It was, as Jessica Simpson might describe it, "Irresistible."

A little later we went back to my apartment. She called me "Kitty," (because she loved cats). She said, "Kitty, can I ask you something?"

I thought, "Please let this be what I think it's going to be."

She said, "I was talking to my sisters and I just want to know, like, how do you feel about me? Like, do you actually like me?"

Was this real?! This was the best question I had ever been asked in my life! This is a common trope in sitcoms and movies. I've seen so many scenes where the guy is thinking, "Oh no, she wants to have 'the talk,'" and he's praying that the woman doesn't start asking, "Where is this going?" or "What *are* we?" In every scene from Hollywood the guy is portrayed as dreading the talk. I didn't dread the talk, are you kidding me? I *loved* the talk. In my head in that moment, fireworks were going off, as I thought, "Hell yes, let's have the talk!" Of course, I didn't let her know that. Plenty of times, I have made the mistake of being the one to initiate this kind of talk. It never worked out well, because that's not the way it's supposed to go. *This* was the way it's supposed to go. The female is supposed to start the conversation. It felt so right and normal.

I hid the excitement from my face, but I thought, "There's no way in hell I'm going to be able to lie with this answer." I did like her! I just had to be confident and own it.

I came back with a casual, "Yeah, I do. I guess your sisters ratted me out?" 😈

I would be lying if I said I wasn't kind of hoping my little confession to her sisters the other day would lead to this. That was partly why I told them. My plan had worked!

She told me that every time we had hung out, the next day she had felt the exact same way I did. Wow, heavy stuff! The moment I got to tell her that I liked her after she asked me was as good as sex! Maybe not as good as meth. Man, I wish I was back there now. That was the perfect whirlwind weekend—but it wasn't over yet.

On Sunday I brought her across town to meet up with her miserable sisters. When we got there, for whatever reason, I could see that once again they both looked very angry. I was halfway home when Krissy called me, crying and upset. She said her sisters had kicked her out of the car and had left without her. She was literally stranded on the side of the road.

I thought, "This is amazing . . . " The weekend just kept getting better, now I got to actually rescue her! Selfishly, I was loving what she was going through because I got to spend more time with her and be the hero. She acted like she didn't want to impose or be a pain in the ass, but I was positively ecstatic to turn around and pick her up from the side of the road.

We got back to my spot, but before long, her wicked sisters showed up. I thought, "Welp, there goes that." But I was awed that they had actually just come back to scream at her some more, make a scene in my parking lot, and then slam the door and peel out. Krissy apologized and asked if it was okay for her to stay with me and, of course, I said it was fine.

Krissy looked at me and said, "Can I tell you something? I really appreciate you being there for me like this all weekend, you're a very special kitty." Everything with her felt so organic, it reminded me of that Selena Gomez song:

Everything comes naturally, it comes naturally
When you're with me, baby

If only she had quoted that to me, I might have gotten down on one knee. Just kidding!

Come Monday, I finally took her to the bus station so she could get back to Dallas. Full disclosure time: this is really embarrassing. I got really emotional. I guess I'll blame it on the meth. When I turned the corner, it hit me that I was really about to drop her off. It had been such an epic weekend, I started tearing up. I reached for my sunglasses and put them on, trying not to give in. I had my face locked like stone, but the tears were coming down my cheeks. I don't know if she noticed, but I can't see how she wouldn't have.

It seemed like every time we hung out, I would get called to work for Edible Arrangements the next day, which was fitting, because Krissy was one hundred percent the girl version of Edible Arrangements. She would come and go, so it never gave me time to screw up.

When I think of Austin, I think of Krissy and Edible Arrangements more than anything else. Well, maybe not more than *Dirty Pop with Lance Bass*. But this story ladies and gentlemen, is why I can't have a normal relationship. I got this emotionally invested in a girl I had hung out with for a grand total of five days! I was literally in tears when I had to drop her off, after five days. I'm just not cut out for this sh*t.

I promise you, if Krissy had lived just down the street from me and it turned into a relationship, it would not have lasted long. There's no doubt that part of my appeal was that I was the guy she couldn't really have, because she only saw me when she was in town. And just like how I never got a chance to get fired from Edible Arrangements, I never had the chance to ruin things with Krissy.

So I can't handle relationships. I can try as hard as possible not to, but I am going to get attached. I'm going to get emotionally invested in anyone I date. I see no getting around it.

A few months later when I left Austin, my sister and her boyfriend Frank flew down to help me pack up my apartment and take a road trip with me back to Maine. I hadn't seen Krissy since that magical weekend, but I thought, "There is no g*ddamn way I'm leaving this state without seeing Krissy again."

Mariah and Frank didn't really want to go through Dallas, but they reluctantly agreed to do it. We went an hour out of our way so I could see Krissy again.

She told me I could come over, but when we got to Dallas, she wasn't picking up her phone, but I knew she wasn't avoiding me. She had given me her address, so we just went there.

We were getting very far behind schedule, and Mariah was getting very annoyed. That's her pet peeve—she likes to be on time for everything. I honestly had no sympathy. My sister has hardly been without a committed relationship since she was fourteen. I thought, "Are you serious? You get to spend this entire road trip, and your life, with the person you love! For God's sake, let me see this incredible girl one last time!" And I thought: "What schedule are we behind on? We are going home for the summer . . . is my sister freaking out over a self-imposed schedule?"

They dropped me off at the front of the complex and I hopped the fence to get in. I walked around the entire property until I found her car, and then I rang every doorbell in the vicinity of the car until, sure enough, one of them woke her up and I got to see her again.

You might picture me going to all these lengths to see a girl again and think it sounds adorable—"What girl wouldn't want that?" But these are not the kinds of things females actually like. I got away with it on this day with Krissy, but normally women want to be the ones doing the chasing. It's quite a difficult spot to be in when you're the kind of guy people *say* women want and not the kind they actually want.

I still wonder sometimes what could have been between Krissy and me, but then I think that I wouldn't have wanted it to end badly. I'll never know if there were long-term possibilities with Krissy, but that's okay. I'll always have my memories of those amazing six days, and that can never be tainted.

Post-Maine Female Friends

Another idea people have about men and women being friends is that they can't be. People like the comedian Steve Harvey say things like, "Ladies, you don't have male friends—you only have guys that want to sleep with you." This is always said from the angle of speaking on behalf of men, while "being brutally honest with the ladies" and "telling women what they don't want to hear."

First of all, what if a girl is unattractive? There goes your theory right there. Unattractive girls usually have great personalities, so it's easy to be friends with them. And yes, I have had female friends that I tried to flirt with when I first met them. But we then became friends and I no longer saw them in sexual terms; I just saw them like a sister.

When people say things like this, I feel it's a veiled attack on men. It's one more stereotype dehumanizing us as sex animals with no emotions, all the while pretending you're speaking on our behalf.

In February 2014 a girl I had randomly friended on Facebook posted a status: "In serious need of a workout buddy, message me if you're interested! Xoxo." I figured she probably posted the status looking for a female workout partner, but I thought maybe I could guilt-trip her into taking up my offer. I wasn't even trying to get with her; I just wanted someone to hang out with. I was in the desert of Utah, and I was kind of back in a friend desert as well. (I was rooming with Jordan at the time, and we were friends, but we weren't best friends by any stretch.)

I said to her, "Are u for real about this workout thing or do u just like to wear the cute gym outfits?"

She then had to say, "Noo I'm serious about it!!"

We agreed to work out together that night. As it turned out, Megan really was about that life. We started going a couple of times a week and it became a real friendship. She liked to complain about people a lot, which I liked. And her thing was: she loved black guys, which I thought was hilarious. She was white, and it wasn't just the whole "black guys have you know what"—it was their style she liked. As weird as it sounds, we definitely bonded over that! I'm not attracted to men obviously, but I could logically understand where she was coming from. A straight white girl and a straight white guy becoming friends over her love of black people: that could only happen to me! 😀

In July of 2015 I was riding around with a friend I had made when I was trying to find gays to be in my music video. Mkiiah Mykels was a locally famous drag queen. As we rode around the east side of Austin, I stopped at a red light and saw two cute black girls on the sidewalk. I yelled out, "Whattup girl!" and one of them looked at me, sized me up, and then she tilted her head to give me a really flirtatious smile as she waved back. I asked if I could get her Facebook before the light turned green, and she started spelling out her name "N-A-N-A . . ." I thought I typed it in right, but when I searched Facebook at the next stop, I couldn't find her! I didn't think she had given me a fake name . . . should I turn around and ask again? Or should I keep driving and never know what could have happened?

I didn't have to deliberate for very long. As I made a U-turn, Mkiiah said, "You really about to turn all the way around for this girl?" "YUP," I replied. I had to! She was exactly the type I wanted to meet, either to get with or just be friends with and introduce me to her other friends. I wanted to hang with some cool, pretty black girls: it was like the final frontier for me. I wanted to find a black Anna! Thank God I'm persistent because I had gotten the spelling wrong! Her name was Nanah! Like my grandmother Nana but with an "H."

However, after she accepted my friend request, I didn't hear anything back from her. Girls think gay men are cool enough as it is, but Mkiiah wasn't just any gay guy, he was a drag queen. I told him, "You've got to add Nanah on Facebook for me and tell her to message me back! I'll owe you big." People love to make fun of me for doing things like that, but it's a concept called "social proof," and it's powerful. After Mkiiah befriended Nanah for me and then told her she should get to know me, I wasn't just a random guy anymore. It was like the owner of the club told the bouncer to let me in, and the velvet rope was unhooked.

The reason I was so insistent was that I knew if I could just get my foot in the door, she'd like me, and Nanah turned out to be one of the best friends I had while I was in Austin. Like I said before, there really were not a lot of young, cool black people in Austin, but Nanah was friends with all of them. She started bringing me to house parties and introduced me to her girlfriends, who all looked like Tia and Tamera Mowry. Nanah was actually half-white, but she loved to go for the *hoodest* black guys, like ones that wore ten chains and . . . well, ones that looked like the guys I was in jail with in Fort Lauderdale! I would let her drive my car, and she would take me riding past her boyfriend's house at 2 a.m. to spy on him. Then I would wait in the car while she ran into the bushes to try to look in his window and see if he was with another girl. (See, it's guys like that, that's what girls want, but will never tell you.) I loved the drama, and I loved that she was bringing me into that world. I don't think Nanah knew any other white guys, so I think I was an exciting novelty for her. I swear, girls who like black guys always seem to like me. And it never would have happened if I was too proud to beg Mkiiah to message her for me.

In Austin with Nanah, September 2015 💯
(Chainz was her boyfriend who got locked up).

Maine: Not the Way My Life Should Be

Fired for My Disability, Summer 2016

So I was back in the good old 207 for my summer gig as a camp counselor. I was sure that Park Lee Camp would be the job that was different. How could it not be? Not only was it a summer camp for people with disabilities, but they hired me *after* seeing my presentation about *my* disability. That's right—they saw the presentation where I talk about how I have been fired from almost every job I've ever had and yet, after hearing all the inside dirt, they still wanted to hire me as a camp counselor. This was like, if a girl heard me speaking on stage about all the personal struggles I've had in my dating experience, and then invited me on a date with her! They even seemed excited to have me because they knew I could relate better to the campers than a neurotypical person could.

I thought, "This will be a great summer. I'll have a chance to be a successful employee for once and get great experience to put on my resume." I thought I would have an easy time making friends, too, and fitting in, since it would all be within a very structured work environment. Lastly, I thought the people there would be understanding and accommodating toward me in social situations.

I went with my dad to check out the campus one day, and some of the counselors I would be working with were hanging out on the lawn. Just in asking some general questions about life as a camp counselor, a few alarm bells went off. I asked if they had a gym on campus or what I could do if I wanted to work out. The answer: they had no gym, and you got virtually no time off for six days a week.

Ever since I had lost eighty pounds a few years before and

pretty much became a walking after-pic of myself, I had made sure I kept working out as an important part of my routine. Going a whole summer without it was not what I signed up for.

These guys seemed cool enough, though, and they were about my age. I kind of wanted to look badass and make an impression on them, so I had my vape and I was taking a few hits off it as we talked, blowing some smoke in the air like it was nothing. 🌀 Of course, it really *was* nothing: it's an electronic device that produces vapor, not actual smoke. Not to mention we were outdoors . . .

I used my vape to quit smoking actual cigarettes and never looked back, as do most people. In Austin, I would puff on it in the airport, and nobody gave a f*ck. Apparently the culture in some places is to lump electronic smoking alternatives into the same category as literal cigarettes, due to the unbearable emotional trauma of seeing something that *looks* like cigarette smoke and smells like a caramel Frappuccino. I was running out of small talk, so I asked what I thought was an obvious question: "It's cool if I have this vape, right?"

They said they weren't going to say anything today, but when camp was in session I wouldn't be allowed to use my e-cig anywhere on campus. They pointed out the designated "smoking" area which was about a mile up the road. I thought they meant I couldn't be hitting the vape indoors (which would have been punitive enough).

They explained adamantly that camp policy was "Absolutely no use of tobacco" anywhere. I'm sorry but sometimes I see a really great chance to subtly point out stupidity and I just can't resist. "I've got a tobacco-free device," I said (seeing as electronic cigarettes don't use tobacco).

"That's camp policy, (sorry-not-sorry)" was their response. It was a moment of politically correct rule-making that I hadn't experienced since I left Maine years before. Living in other parts of the country, I have found that there is less of this kind of "sweating the small stuff" attitude that I find whenever I go back to the Northeast.

And smoke on this: people are always eager to tell you about how bad smoking is for you. But if we really cared about the dangers of smoking, then we wouldn't be subjecting people who have opted for a healthier alternative to the same inconveniences inflicted on smokers. *Mic drop*

I know there's a negative stereotype of people who vape, but I do it because I like it. It chills me out; it gives me something to do. Many people on the spectrum feel comfortable if they have something they can always carry around with them, like a "fidget toy." Now they're telling me I have to walk a mile all summer if I want to vape? And I'm screwed if I want to exercise in a gym? It might be a lot easier to just lie on my resumes!

These guys did, however, tell me one awesome thing . . . about half of the counselors were going to be British. I don't know why every summer camp has a ton of British counselors, but I love British people. They're smart, they have that dry British sense of humor, and in my experience Brits will talk pop music with you for days. I've always said the person with the best taste in music ever would be a gay, black, British guy. For all I knew there could be a gay, black, British guy who decided to take a summer job in Maine, so I wasn't taking any chances!

I arrived for the first day of training a few weeks later. When I got there, everybody was playing a friendly game of kickball. I actually don't mind playing sports. It's watching them that I can't wrap my head around. I got in the outfield and quickly made friends with a bloke who was so British, I knew it before he spoke. If you just close your eyes and picture a British guy, I guarantee you've got him. Just wait for his name, though—it was pronounced "Allister" but spelled "Alasdair." I'm not making fun—this is what I wanted, remember? Alasdair was a cool dude, and I wish everyone there had been as nice as he was.

We were switching back and forth between standing in line to kick and being in the field as I thought to myself, "This is so trippy, these are my coworkers I'm playing kickball with, not my classmates in Phys ed." It didn't feel like a job; it felt like waking up in a childhood memory. If you've read *Chasing the Rabbit,* you know that no one would want to wake up in my childhood! This would be a common theme over the next two weeks.

I had assumed that since this was a job, it would be very structured. In most jobs that have a heavy social aspect, everybody gets to know everybody else in a controlled environment. If this helps, imagine the high school cafeteria . . . now picture the complete opposite of that. All the painful, cringe-y, social challenges of fending for yourself in the jungle that is a school cafeteria are eliminated—and replaced with order and predictability. Every challenge of making friends is neutralized in the workplace, because none of us make the schedule!

Ask anyone on the spectrum or anyone even just a little socially awkward, and I promise you they all love the workplace environment for this exact reason. If you can believe it, I'm never as comfortable anywhere as I am in the workplace. For someone with autism, that structure is like finding an island of peace while a war is going on everywhere else.

I thought working as a camp counselor would hand me that kind of social interaction on a silver platter, because I would be spending a whole summer with people my age, and just from researching the place there seemed to be a heavy emphasis on everybody being friends! You've got to admire my optimism, right? Instead, what I got was a Wild, Wild West of high-school-cafeteria-style chaos.

First off, it was apparent to me that half of my fellow counselors didn't like me almost from the start. Some people, I'm convinced, just get a vibe from me that rubs them the wrong way on a visceral level. It isn't even a conscious thing, which is why they can tell you to your face they have no problem with you, and in their mind, that's the truth! Meanwhile, I've learned a thing or two about reading people, and as soon as I say two words to people like that, it's almost like they're in physical pain just trying to be polite to me.

In terms of socializing, there was no structure whatsoever. Talk to anyone who struggles socially in school, especially if they have autism, and they will tell you they *hate* it when teachers say, "All right, everybody partner up!" In fact, I think this is a practice that should be outlawed.

This was essentially the framework of the entire week of training. Now I don't mind the whole sink-or-swim, make-friends-or-be-an-outcast setup if maybe I'm at a nightclub or a house party. In those situations, I don't expect to be included without putting in some work. But not only was this a *job*, it was a job helping people with disabilities. *And they knew I had one, too.*

Now, *because of my disability*, I was in situations where there would be six or seven people all walking in a tight huddle five feet away from me, laughing with each other, just blatantly excluding me. Nobody should have to experience that in a workplace whose oft-repeated mantra is, "We're all friends at Park Lee Camp!" If you asked me to how to make sure that someone with autism would easily and quickly fail at a job, I would say, "Go watch Park Lee Camp training week."

What made it worse was that this was the kind of politically correct environment I hadn't been in since I was a kid in elementary school. It was clear to me really quickly that these people all had a similar worldview: "Stereotypes are evil." Not just stereotypes, though—making any kind of generalization about the world, no matter how obvious it was.

For example, "Black people are good at dancing," would be considered a hateful thing to say. I understand the good intentions behind this way of thinking and all, but it makes it very hard for me to have any kind of conversation because of how my mind works. It's part of my autism that I have very rigid, black-and-white ways of thinking. As you may have gathered by now, I tend to see the world in terms of categories, and that includes people, too. I see the world as, "These people do this, those people do that, etc." And I believe that recognizing our differences is celebrating diversity. When I'm not allowed to make even the most mundane observations about the world without being condemned, it's a really incompatible culture for me to fit into.

A perfect example of this clash in worldviews: I went with a group of counselors up the road to the designated smoking area. A younger Dielawn would not have accepted the outlandish policy of having to vape in the smoking area, but luckily, by twenty-four I was mature enough to go with it and take the opportunity to bond with some of my coworkers. Remember the "cig convo?" I have no problem with cigarettes, I smoked them for years. One guy pulled out a pack of Newports, so unsurprisingly I said, "Newports— nice, that's what black people smoke." I said this with a smile, so he knew I was being friendly. But he couldn't accept the "evil stereotype" that I had apparently just expressed with my harmless (and very true) statement!

"Do they?" he snapped back, "I know black people who smoke Marlboros. I know black people who smoke American Spirits." Someone else felt the need to chime in with, "I know black people that smoke Pall Malls!" *Man oh man! Were these guys serious?* I played it cool, but in my head I was flipping. By the way, I promise you, *any* black person will verify that Newports are overwhelmingly the choice of African-American smokers. There was nothing correct about this political correctness! If only there had been any black people in the group, you can best believe they would have backed me up one hundred percent. 💯 But it wasn't worth it; all I could do was shake my head and let it drop.

If you know me at all, or if you know others with high-functioning autism, you know that letting things drop is not our strength in any way. We're usually the complete opposite, especially when we *know* we're right. It took every ounce of my strength to let that conversation drop and let these diversity-hating stereotype police feel like they had won.

Now, I hate snitches. I never want to be that guy who runs to human resources behind your back. I feel ratting people out is dishonorable. But if there's one lesson I've learned in the workplace, it's that when you're at work, the rules are "snitch or get snitched on." I can't count the number of times I've been shocked to find out that coworkers who acted like friends to my face, had been covertly reporting me to HR. I saw an opportunity here to finally use the system that had been used against me so many times. And if I could use it to guilt people into not treating me poorly for no reason? Oh yeah, I was all over this. Don't get it twisted though—I told them nothing but the truth. I told them that because my disability is not what people are used to seeing, I was being treated poorly by the majority of my coworkers. It felt great to take a stand for myself, and honestly, it felt even better because these people had sat around all week professing how much they all cared about accommodating people's special needs. Well, what if one's special need is to be included in social interactions?

Park Lee Camp told me that informing everybody about the specifics of my disability was not the way they liked to do things because, as a summer camp, their goal was for this to be the one place people can come every year to forget about their disabilities., and just be treated as normal. I pushed back with a concept I knew would be hard for them to swallow. I insisted, "That policy works for individuals whose disability is visible, and there's no need to talk about it. My disability is literally invisible unless you tell people, and my situation is the exact inverse. I have to live 99 percent of my life like I don't have a disability. I would love for Park Lee Camp to be the one place I get treated like I'm disabled."

I implored them to throw confidentiality out the window for me! Let all my coworkers know my business! One other thing I've learned is that if I'm trying to keep a job, I don't mind being treated by everybody like I'm "special." I guess it really is the opposite of middle school!

To Park Lee Camp's credit and my surprise, they reluctantly agreed to do it! They went around to every cabin and did exactly what I had requested. And to my credit—and probably their surprise—it worked! The next day at breakfast, I was sitting with a group of counselors as they were talking about cultural differences in the U.S. versus England. When I chimed in, they actually welcomed me into the conversation! They treated me like a friend, as opposed to an outsider they had to be polite to. The rest of the day was just like that: a total one-eighty, like I was at a different place. What a huge wave of relief! The guilt-tripping of my counselors translated into me being given a chance as a person. It really was social affirmative action! Or social socialism.

It's too bad I waited so long to advocate for myself, because the next day I got fired for something I never expected to be my downfall.

As an adult, I had become used to taking my own meds as part of a regular routine. When I was unpacking on opening day, I was looking at a checklist the camp had given everybody and it said something about disclosing all our medications to the nurse's office. My parents were with me, so I asked them if I should do that. Trying to be helpful, they told me, "Don't worry about that, some things you can just keep to yourself." I agreed because it was embarrassing enough that I had to take some of these meds. I didn't want to have them given to me every day by some strange, fifty-year-old nurse.

So, I kept my meds on my dresser, next to my bed. After about two weeks, the head counselor said, "Dylan, you should probably give those to the nurse, because they don't want us having medications out in the cabin like that." I said okay and figured I would do it when I got around to it. Apparently, what he should have said was, "Dylan, if you don't bring those to the nurse's office right now, you will be fired tomorrow morning!" Because that's exactly what happened. Their defense was that they had "warned" me. Well, yes, technically they had. During the course of a week-long orientation that included many hours of seminars, they mentioned it. But like everybody, I pay attention the best I can and, as you know by now, I don't retain one hundred percent of the information given to me.

This is especially true when the seminar that included this little tidbit was prefaced by the nurse herself, saying, "I'm sorry this is gonna bore you guys, but I legally have to tell you this stuff, so bear with me!" And true to her disclaimer, most of it was stuff I didn't need to pay attention to, like "Make sure to apply sunscreen" and "How not to get AIDS." Of course I pulled out my phone and got on Facebook; are you kidding me? She basically told us we didn't have to pay attention! I thought this was the equivalent of the flight attendant demonstrating how to use the oxygen masks!

But hey, if I was going to get fired from this job, I was happy it was a technicality like that instead of something behavioral where I actually screwed up.

My dad was very angry about this firing. He called the people he knew at the camp and asked why I had been fired with no warning. They said, "We did warn him. He was told just the day before that he should probably bring his meds to the nurse's office."

My dad responded, "Are you kidding me? You know he has autism and that people with autism take everything literally. The words 'should' and 'probably' are suggestive words, so when you gave him that so-called warning, he heard it as a suggestion!"

I told my dad I didn't *hear* this as a suggestion, this *was* a suggestion. And one thing about my literal interpretation of words: from watching cable news debates, I've noticed that whenever you neurotypicals want to be right, you will jump over to my way of thinking real quick. All of a sudden, everything a politician said, he or she *had to mean literally*. My autistic understanding of words helps you guys whenever you want to prove a point. Can we talk some royalties?

A couple of weeks later, they agreed to meet with me. They admitted, "We did what you describe in your book talks. We underestimated your disability." It is such a reoccurring theme: because of my presentation skills, people assume that my autism "isn't that bad." They assume it doesn't impact every single thing I do in my life. They are so wrong! And because of that assumption, I disappoint almost everyone I meet.

Stuck in Maine

Before I was fired from the camp, I genuinely intended that leaving Texas for my new start in Maine would mean the end of doing drugs. I'd had my fun times, but it was time to stop. I couldn't do meth the rest of my life, and I had no interest in becoming a drug addict.

The first couple of weeks back in Maine were great. I was getting along with my family, and Maine seemed to be giving me the fresh start that I never expected there. Maine had always felt like a complete dead end for me, but I had gone off to camp with the highest hopes for a great summer. When I was fired out of nowhere just when things seemed to be going much better for me there, the summer—and my life—really took a nosedive. I had returned to Maine for that job, and now I'd lost the reason for being there. Now I was simply back in Maine—drifting aimlessly.

My dad made me start working in his factory. I grudgingly did it while complaining about it. At first, I was thinking, "This sucks," but it wasn't actually that bad because there was a young guy my age who was pretty cool and took to me. There was also a black guy there who grew up in the '80s, so guess what we talked about. Those guys were fun, even though the job itself did kind of suck.

Overall I was *so bored* that summer, and no matter what anybody wanted to tell me, how could I not feel like a huge failure after going from being a camp counselor to working in my family's factory?

I started talking to TJ, one of the gay guys I knew from Austin. He was a big time meth dealer, older than I was, maybe thirty-five. I'd hung out with him one time when I took too much G. I was falling all over the place and didn't know what was going on, and I even pissed myself. I know G is sometimes used to take advantage of people, but he didn't do that at all. I remember him carrying me to a bathtub and trying to get me to rinse off, basically babysitting me. So, understandably, I saw him as someone I could trust.

I messaged TJ, asking him how he was doing and saying that I wished I hadn't left Austin. We started reminiscing on the good times doing drugs at his house and listening to Jump Smokers remixes of pop songs. Then, he offered to send me some meth. He said he had done this before with other people and assured me it was safe.

TJ said he'd give me a really good deal. All I had to do was PayPal him a hundred dollars, and in a few days, I'd have enough ice to last me for weeks.

At first I told him that was ridiculous, I didn't even consider it. But then a couple more weeks went by, and things in Maine got more and more miserable. I wasn't doing anything with my life except working in a box factory, eating constantly, and gaining weight as I do whenever I'm unhappy. So I told TJ, "F*ck it—send me some meth!"

I have to be honest: writing about this makes me want to do meth again right now. That feeling of not caring about anything was what I found most addicting about meth. After a lousy summer getting fired from camp and having to work for my dad like I was sixteen again, not having a care in the world sounded pretty damn good.

The meth arrived. I wish I could tell you the story, but for legal reasons that's as much detail as I can give you. 😂 On my way to work, I pulled into Sedgefield Downs, a local harness racing track that's usually just a big empty parking lot. Up to that point, I had never done meth on my own. In Austin, I'd just done it partying with other people. I did a line; I did two lines. In about ten minutes, it was like I'd entered another dimension, like I was in a new reality. I was blasting my favorite Madonna songs and having the time of my life! The best part was that as I went about my day, I was in my own private fantasy world, and no one had to know.

My life felt pointless at that time. The only thing I had going for me was my local radio show, but of course you don't make much money doing that, and it was only once a week. And remember how terrified I was at the thought of not being able to go to the gym for the summer? Well, now I'd thrown out my shoulder lifting weights, and I was about to go in for a rotator cuff surgery that would leave me unable to lift weights for no less than *nine months*. On top of that, during this time I was combating a thyroid issue, which my doctor and I had been trying to get under control. You know the God-awful groggy feeling you have the first few minutes after you get out of bed in the morning? Because of the thyroid issue, I felt like that all day long. But with meth, I had a magic wand that made all of it disappear.

After I did it that first day, I had never been so happy to go work in the factory. The thing about meth is: it enables you to be very focused on simple physical tasks, so it was perfect for stacking boxes on an assembly line. On my break I went and grabbed the stereo system from the gym and carried it out to set it up in the plant. It was a late-night shift, so nobody cared. I turned work into a box assembly-slash-DJ gig. I was playing all my favorite Janet Jackson and Bobby Brown tracks for the black guy I worked with so he could relive his childhood. There are few things I love more than watching people react as I play songs they remember from their past. But I never would have been happy enough to do all that sober.

I started doing meth every day. Of course, when you're on meth, you can stay up for days at a time; sometimes I'd even be up a whole week! It really makes you superhuman. I was eating just enough to not be sick, like a single hardboiled egg for the whole day. For me, food has always been the drug I've wrestled with, and in a way it's the worst vice to have because you can't just quit. With my autism, I would love it if food was a black and white issue: something I could just not do, period. It drives me crazy that with the thing I struggle with most, I have to find this awkward gray area of doing it just enough, but not too much. It's like if an alcoholic had to drink in moderation every day. The experience of not having the thought of food even enter my consciousness was the most freeing thing I had ever known. My life may have been a mess, but I felt like it was a controlled mess. And at least I wasn't getting fat.

Maine N' Meth

The fall of 2016 was a dizzying, up-and-down ride, depending on whether or not I could get hold of a meth supply. I was in a sling recovering from my surgery and attending physical therapy. There would be a couple of weeks where I'd be running around all happy, doing meth every day. I'd be smiling, getting along great with my family and full of life. Then there'd be a couple of weeks when I'd be waiting for more. Going from being high and carefree to being hungry again, dealing with thyroid issues and in a sling unable to work out, was such a face plant back into reality, I'd end up sleeping most of the day to escape it.

Without meth, when I was awake I'd eat everything I could get my hands on. It went like this:

1. *I feel depressed that I want to eat again, so to feel better, I eat.*
2. *I feel fat after I eat.*
3. *I feel depressed some more.*
4. *I eat some more.*
5. *Now I'm already fat, might as well keep eating.*

It's a vicious cycle I know all too well. I knew this was self-destructive behavior, but in the back of my mind, I also knew that as soon I got more meth, the pounds would fall right back off. And I wasn't wrong. When TJ would finally get around to sending me more meth it was like I went from lying on the ground, not having the energy to pick myself up, glued to a nasty, unswept floor . . . and then I would do a line and it was like a hot air balloon came and swooped me up off the ground, and I went from lying in the dirt to skydiving.

The drugs were fun to do when it was warm out. But in Maine, after Thanksgiving it's too cold to be outside. And the days get very short in December: it's pitch black by 4:00 p.m., freezing cold, and often snowy.

I couldn't do my regular routine of getting high and then blasting music in the house, although a few times I did. But most of the time I had to get out of the house. In warm weather, getting outside was no problem: I could just drive around with my windows down and chill wherever. Now that it was the dead of winter, I had to focus on going from indoor place to indoor place, which was a lot trickier.

I scouted out all the best hotels in the area, looking for places with a lobby that had a one-person restroom with really nice marble counters. I'd walk in like I was staying there and nod to the people at the desk. The lobby restroom is usually away from the front desk, out of sight. If it wasn't, I'd walk the halls and circle back around and hit the restroom on the way out.

Once I was in there, I'd get my ice out and do lines off the counters, making the nice, clean hotel restroom my own little drug getaway. I'd either play my music or listen to talk radio, such as *The Alan Colmes Show,* just loud enough to enjoy but not loud enough to draw attention to the restroom. I bet I'm literally the only person who's ever done meth while listening to Alan Colmes (rest in peace).

Going to hotel bathrooms started to feel like a lifestyle, not just a thing I did. Everything revolved around getting out of the house and going to get high. It started taking longer and longer and, after a while, it started feeling lame. Using meth went from being fun, like it was in Texas, to making me feel like a total loser: a loser who drives to the Holiday Inn Express to pretend I'm staying there, just to sneak in the restroom to do some lines.

The thing with meth is that it gives you this electrifying surge of energy, and you don't want to sit still. I really needed a place where I could run around and jam out to my music without anybody noticing how unusually energetic I was. Once it was too cold to be outside, I staked out my new hangout in the gym at the factory, where I could use the loud stereo system. I would go there for entire nights. This was my new safe haven, a peaceful place where I could be alone and just be high. Sometimes I'd bring people with me, but I honestly liked being there alone. I'd blast my music and do line after line in the locker room, and just create a party for myself that felt more like a party than just about any party I've ever been to.

It wasn't typical of me to prefer being alone; after all, I've spent my whole life working so hard to have friends. I was always chasing that damn rabbit. But when I did meth, the rabbit could go f*ck itself! I loved that feeling; it was so liberating. Meth is the only drug I know of that's more fun to do by yourself. It made being alone an adventure. A sad, pathetic adventure? Maybe, but an adventure nonetheless.

New Old Friends

One cool thing about being back in Maine was that my old friend Anna still lived there, so I could hang out with her. Years ago I'd had a crush on her, but that was long gone. She was dating this guy Matt, whom I used to know back in the day too, and I was glad she ended up with him. They're adorable together, and I was still friendly with him, too.

Once upon a time we all used to hangout, and I really wanted to be friends with both of them again, but especially Anna. My reasoning was that I felt like while I was living in Maine, if we couldn't go back to hanging out on a regular basis, it would retro-actively delegitimize whatever friendship we'd once had.

We did hang out a few times, but it wasn't enough for me. It upset me that I couldn't go back to the way things were. I wanted to go back to the days when she would hit me up every day and we'd do everything together. You might be thinking, "Oh, the boyfriend didn't want you to." That wasn't even it though. Matt and I were cool with each other, and he was usually there, too.

My theory is that, when someone changes a lot from the person you used to know, and you aren't there to witness the gradual change, it can strike you as very strange. It can almost come off very fake and unnatural, because you didn't see the process of them changing. Or maybe it was a simple case of out of sight, out of mind, and she'd just moved on.

I'd hit her up every now and then, figuring that if I had to try too hard, she didn't want to be friends that much. One thing I absolutely didn't want was to start begging or coming off desperate; I'd rather just not be friends with her than try to force a friendship that wasn't there anymore.

That's not to say I'm always good at resisting the urge to try too hard, I make that mistake *a lot*. But it's funny—sometimes when you care the most, the game becomes the easiest. When you truly value someone, sometimes you throw all the bullsh*t aside and do what you're supposed to do.

The times we did hang out, we always had a great time. It was even better now that we were both grown up. When you're a teenager, it's not cool to flaunt your intelligence. So even if you are smart underneath, which I could always tell she was, you almost have to hide it and just focus on fitting in. Once you're in your twenties, suddenly it's okay to be smart. And I really liked this new, adult Anna, I felt like she had become who she was. I think there will always be a special place in my heart for her as a friend and just as a person. If you knew her, there probably would be too! If not, then you're probably lame. 😆

One of my Best Choices, December 2016

In March 2016 my dad and I were speaking to an audience of about five hundred people in Richmond, Virginia. My favorite part of the presentation is always the Q&A, for moments just like this. A woman raised her hand and asked me, "What would you do if you had a child with autism?"

Without hesitation I said, "That's why I'm saving up for a vasectomy!"

The audience erupted in laughter, but I wasn't kidding. Later that night, my dad said, "Hey, that thing you said today about getting a vasectomy . . . were you serious?"

I said, "Oh yeah, I was one hundred percent serious! Having a kid would be the worst thing that could ever happen to me. Worse than getting fired from any job, worse than going to jail—a kid is prison! What if I had a kid with a disability? What if I had a low-functioning autistic kid that I had to support the rest of my life? I can barely support myself, I'm gonna support a kid?!"

My dad didn't have much to say to that. How was he going to argue with my logic? And then I laid on something I knew would lock up his support. "You know my type of girls," I said. "Any girl I knocked up wouldn't come from a stable family. So, I'd be unable to care for a kid, and you and Mom would never be able to let your grandchild be raised in a bad home, so who would really get screwed? Do you and Mom want to start over with a baby at fifty?"

I was twenty-five, so time was running out for me to remain on my parents' health insurance plan. I told my dad it was absolutely a green light on my end, so he went ahead and made me an appointment. When I told the primary care doctor what I wanted to do, he refused to give me a referral and claimed that no doctor would ethically perform a vasectomy on someone my age that had no children. I was very frustrated that he was unwilling to listen to what I thought was my mature and logically sound reasoning.

Fortunately, my dad knew another doctor who might be willing to help me out. When I saw this other doctor, I explained my rationale, and it made sense to him. He said he appreciated my maturity and gave me the referral.

A couple of weeks later, I was in the urologist's office getting snipped. It was pretty easy! My dad definitely took it harder than I did. He was very emotional knowing that I would never be a father. He loves being a dad, so he was upset that I would never experience it. I never gave it a thought; I knew it was the right decision for me.

I find the whole idea of reproduction thoroughly unappealing. Making photocopies of myself, and then watching these little humans walk around that are half me . . . jacking my facial features, ripping off my swag?! It's like copyright infringement. There's only one of me. I'm a registered trademark.™

If, and that's a big if, I ever do decide to have kids, I like the idea of adoption. Any issues the kid has, you know it's not a mess you made. I could do my best to help and give the child a good upbringing, but all while knowing it's not my genes that got us here. 😵 I like the idea of being the solution, not the problem.

Anyway, why have kids when you can have cats? There is no child that could ever be as beautiful as a cat. I look forward to a life of cat fatherhood; my dream is to someday fill a house with ten adult cats!

I was excited four months later when the follow-up test confirmed that I was "shooting blanks." Now I could relax when I was with a girl because I knew there was no way she could get pregnant. That I escaped ever causing a pregnancy and got a vasectomy are two rare victories in my life. Whenever I'm having a bad day, I think about those two things, and it brings me up a little. 😃

Anna's Birthday, January 2017

On Saturday night, January 7, 2017, as I was leaving the house, my dad said the same thing he said to me every night: "Make good decisions."

Earlier that day I had messaged Anna; the next night was her birthday, and I hadn't been seeing her much. You know how sometimes you wait a while to say something, and then the timing just feels right? On impulse I opened up Facebook and asked her in what I thought was an appropriately assertive but not too try-hard way, "What is it with you lately? You weren't always like this."

Apparently I did something right, because she started apologizing; she told me she always had a blast when we hung out, and she'd love to have me there for her birthday! My plan had worked! But from there, the plan for that night got a little confusing. We were supposed to go out bar-hopping, but she also mentioned that we needed a place to party at. Wanting to be the hero, I said we could party at my dad's office. She told me, "That's perfect," and asked me if I could get some people, especially girls, to come and party with us.

Anna knew me back when I had a lot more issues socially. Over the years as I matured, I gained a new appreciation for how lucky I was that she was willing to associate with me back then, through all the cringe-y social faux pas I made. Regardless of why she did it, she still did it. This is where it comes back to the concept of validating someone's choice to befriend me. I feel like the best way to reward someone for their friendship is to vindicate their decision by proving them right. In other words, I wanted to impress her by being able to bring people to her party.

However, I really hadn't been going out and meeting people that much. I had been spending most of my time on meth, in my own world. Now I had just volunteered to get a whole group of guys and girls to come party with us at an industrial park in Biddeford. I had to figure something out, I couldn't come up empty-ended. There was a guy from South Portland named Logan I had hung out with a couple of times. He was twenty-one, and he had two girls and two guys that we could go pick up to come party for the night. The problem was, one of the girls and one of the guys were nineteen and twenty. I was so happy I had found a group of people on such short notice, it didn't even occur to me that they would all have to all be twenty-one to go bar-hopping with us.

I had all five of them in my car on the way to Biddeford when Anna texted me about which bar to go to. Damnit. Now I was in a bind. I couldn't separate the group I had picked up and just tell the nineteen- and twenty-year-olds to wait on the side of the road for us. Not following my dad's advice, I made a snap decision instead of a good one. I decided I would drop them off at Volk Packaging, let them in and then, after Anna and I hit the bars, we'd meet back up with them. I figured, "I'll give them the Wi-Fi password, set them up with music, and leave them to do whatever they want. How mad could they be?"

I had hung out with this group once before, and they all seemed like nice enough kids. I wasn't worried they were going to burn the place down or steal anything. I was one hundred percent worried about impressing Anna and wanted the night to go well.

Anna had a friend named Cathy who didn't really like me. In fact, she didn't really like anyone. She reminded me of one of those cats at the shelter that hisses at everyone and never gets adopted.

When I picked Anna up, she said, "Cathy is begging for us to go pick her up, but we don't have to—I really don't care." I should have taken the hint and not picked her up, but I wanted to be nice, so I picked up Cathy and her boyfriend and brought them with us.

I should have known Cathy would hog Anna's attention the whole night, but nevertheless we still had a pretty good time. I didn't drink much, because after all, I was already on meth. We'd been at the bar for about two hours, and then Anna started getting into an argument on Snapchat with her boyfriend Matt, who had stayed home, so we left.

Knowing Anna was drunk, for some reason I still let her drive. I have no idea why I did that, since being on meth gives you no problems focusing on the road, not to mention it was dark and snowing! I think it was just another case of me looking at neuro-typical people as God. Since I know I'm very bad at making deci-sions, I'll often hang my hat on every word neurotypical people say and take it as gospel. Anna said she was good to drive, so I thought she must know better than me.

Then I realized she was driving straight home, meanwhile the people I had dropped off at Volk Packaging had been blowing up my phone asking where we were. I felt like she was screwing me over, but she was tired and fed up with the boyfriend drama and just wanted to go home instead of going to party more. I was really disappointed.

We were in the middle of nowhere on a winding road near Anna's house when the car spun out of control and crashed into a snowbank, where it got stuck.

First thing I did was say, "All right, we're fine, we're fine."

She yelled at me, "Really, are we fine?!"

I called AAA, but they said they were backed up because of the snowstorm and wouldn't be able to get to us for two hours.

Next, Anna tried calling her mother for help, since we were only five minutes from her house. Her mom hung up the phone on her. She was going to just leave her daughter stranded on the side of the road in a snowbank, on her birthday much less. I can't imagine what it would be like to have a parent like that. As many times as I have screwed up in my life, whenever I'm in real trouble or danger, my parents are there for me. It looked like this might be another one of those times. The problem was that it was 2:00 a.m., and I had no idea what to tell them. Also, there were a bunch of people at the factory, waiting to get picked up.

To make matters worse, Anna and Matt were still arguing; we were running low on gas; and it was ten degrees outside. Anna started getting hysterical and panicking in a way I'd never seen before. I always knew that she had some issues, but I never really saw them. She kept saying, "I want to go home. I want to go home."

I was trying to calm her down and comfort her. That took some empathy, which I sometimes have a very hard time showing. Many of us with autism find it difficult to see things from someone else's perspective, a skill that would have come in handy at a time like that.

Or perhaps it might have been that I saw things too much from her perspective, and I didn't know how to sugarcoat it. Did I need to fake a cool, calm, confident voice and somehow tell her this wasn't so bad? I can't fake emotions, and I don't know the right things to say. I was trying, but not doing it well, so I chuckled and said, "I suck at this."

She laughed (in the middle of crying hysterically) and said, "Me too." It was things like that, see—that's what made her cool.

I took that as a cue that maybe I could try to lighten the mood. There were a lot of songs that Anna and I used to jam to, back in 2009 and 2010, and they bring back great memories. One of our songs used to be "Carry Out" by Timbaland and Justin Timberlake, and I had a feeling it was one that got left in 2010. I played it, and she said, "Oh my God, I literally haven't heard this song since we hung out in high school."

That was pretty great, but we weren't in high school anymore. We were adults, and we were in a dark, sh*tty moment. I got out and tried to get the car out of the snowbank, but I couldn't budge it. I was embarrassed because I knew it looked bad that I couldn't move it, but really the thing was so buried, not even the Hulk could have moved it. There was a house nearby, and someone came out and tried to help me move it, but still no luck. Anna finally decided to call a cab. She invited me to go with her if I wanted, but I decided to stay with the car.

When she left in the cab, I moved into the driver's seat. It seemed weird sitting in the passenger's seat when there was no one else in the car, why wouldn't I sit in the driver's seat while waiting for AAA?

I should have just left with her. About ten minutes later, some cops pulled up. Someone who saw the car stuck in the snowbank must have called the police to be "helpful." They didn't want to stop and help, that would have been *too* helpful. Apparently they must have thought I didn't have a cell phone in the year 2017.

Another Run-In with the Law

When the cops showed up, I didn't think it was a big deal. In my mind, I hadn't done anything wrong. Can you imagine thinking I didn't do anything wrong? That's the way my brain works. From the time I was in kindergarten, I could never tell when I'd done something wrong. My life has been like walking through a forest blindfolded, and trying not to bump into trees. With neurotypical people, it's like you're not blindfolded: you see the trees and you walk around them. Meanwhile I just keep feeling my head bash into the bark. I can realize I'm in a situation that's not good for me, but that's a lot different than seeing the big picture of what led me there. As I write this, I can think of so many times when I was in a bad place, but I'm still not sure what I could have done differently, knowing only what I knew at the time.

The police started questioning me like I'd done something wrong. They asked me to get out of the car and take sobriety tests. Apparently, I failed them all. They said because the car was running, it meant that technically I was "operating" the vehicle. I was just trying to stay warm.

I knew I hadn't actually been the one driving, so it seemed like they were being complete jerks to me. This was definitely a case of me not being able to empathize with other people's perspectives. I find empathy especially challenging when I know the other person has his or her facts wrong. To look past the inaccuracies and see their point of view is virtually impossible for me.

I tried telling them what happened with Anna and her friends, but looking at me on the side of the road by myself; it seemed to them like an implausible story. In my mind, if anything is going to be black and white, it should be the law. I didn't care how crazy my "story" seemed, it was the truth. And I bet if I had been a girl who was abandoned by a guy, the police would have believed me.

I told them that after the girl driving left, I didn't want to sit in the passenger's seat by myself and freeze my ass off while waiting for AAA, so of course I had the car running for heat.

They said I should have called the police to report the crash and called someone to come get me instead of running my car, because even having the car on in park was considered Operating Under the Influence (OUI). I wanted to scream at them, "I didn't anticipate having to plan for laws that say running your car in park is *drunk driving!*"

I realized they believed I'd done more than just have the car running, so they were trying to nail me with this technicality. Obviously no reasonable person is going to be waiting for AAA in ten degree weather and turn off the car. I saw this as an abuse of logic, and it really rustled me.

I'd had like a drink and a half back at the bar. But that had been a couple of hours earlier, so I wasn't sure whether or not I would be over the legal limit. I had, however, failed the sobriety tests. Mostly I think because it was ten degrees out, and there was also the meth, but maybe I was still feeling some of the effects of the alcohol.

The police wanted me to take the breathalyzer test. This is where all my time spent listening to talk radio shows paid off. I'd heard from a segment on *The Tom Leykis Show* that the cops' game is to intimidate and manipulate you into believing you have to do the breathalyzer. I was 99 percent sure I didn't have to actually do it. If you refuse, they take you in and do a blood test at the station. By the time they get through all the paperwork, it can buy you an extra couple of hours, thanks to the efficiency of our government.

I used my best argument skills, giving them the runaround, trying to kill time and annoy them enough so that they would just take me in. Eventually I talked my way out of the breathalyzer, but they decided they were going to detain me anyway on suspicion of drunk driving. As I sat down in the back of the squad car, they asked if I had any belongings I'd like them to retrieve before they searched my car.

Of course, what they hadn't found yet was a little black case that came with my Beats headphones, inside of which were my drugs. I'd left it sitting right on the passenger's seat.

What I did next has been characterized by many as comically stupid of me. That people didn't understand why I made this next move upset me almost as much as getting arrested. It's a recurring scenario I've run into all my life. Because of the way my mind works, operating from a formula of past experiences plus logical calculations, rather than intuition like most people, sometimes my actions appear foolish before hearing out my reasoning. That's because my actions go against many people's gut feelings, whereas many people's gut feelings would go against my logic.

I've had my car searched before, and let me tell you they look in every nook and cranny. The police will open up your spare wheel compartment to shine a flashlight in there! But I've also been to jail before, and I can tell you that the law is full of nuances and gray areas in terms of what your rights are, which of your possessions the police can search, certain containers they're allowed to look inside, certain items they can't open . . . the law is complex.

So I made a calculation. If I asked them to retrieve this bag for me, there might be some loophole, some technicality I don't know about, where they wind up not opening this ziplocked Beats case. I mean hell, who would have thought running your car for heat on the side of the road while waiting for AAA could land you an OUI? It was pretty unlikely, but the alternative as I saw it, was a *one-hundred-percent certainty* they find it in five seconds of searching my car. So I made a hail-mary pass, and asked them to bring me my Beats case.

When they opened it up and found the meth, I can't say I was shocked. It was a one-hundred percent chance they find it, or a 99 percent chance, either way my odds weren't great. So at first glance, people thought it was stupid that I "asked the cops for my drugs," but if only life was a debate stage, confetti would rain down over my logic every time.

At the station, they did a preliminary test and came back to tell me it was heroin. I said, "Are you sure?"

One of the cops said, "Yes, our tests are one hundred percent accurate."

I thought, "Okay, this will be easy," because I definitely don't do heroin.

Then they did another test, and this time it came back as meth. I was really tempted to say, "What about your hundred percent accurate test?" but I held back, figuring it wasn't the best time to start being a smartass. Though I promise you a Dielawn of the past would have taken the jab.

The police had called my parents, who were now waiting in the lobby of the station. As you can imagine, they were pissed and—that word parents love to use—*disappointed* in me. The arresting officer went out to them and said, "Well, I have good news and bad news. The good news is that he tested at zero-point-five, so he was not legally driving drunk. The bad news is that we found these drugs in his car. We think it's methamphetamine."

I was being arrested for possession of crystal meth. My parents flipped out; this was their ultimate nightmare scenario. They came back to where I was and told me how disappointed they were but that they loved me. I tried to feign shock that the drugs were found in my car; it's amazing how drugs have the power to turn you into such a liar. And you have no conscience about it, because the drugs come before all else. Not that I didn't lie to my parents without the drugs, but with the handcuffs on, acting like I didn't know how this shiny rock got in my car—that took some chutzpa.

Then I told them about the people at Volk Packaging, waiting for me to come back and pick them up. I don't know what my dad was thinking at that moment, but I can guarantee it was nothing good. He had trusted me with a key to his office, and I had violated that trust. He later told me that was almost as bad as being caught with drugs. He was even more pissed when he later arrived at the factory to find the place a mess, reeking of cigarettes and weed.

At the police station, they told me not to smile in my mugshot, they said, "It's a mugshot—it doesn't matter."

I thought, "Are you kidding me? Everyone I know is going to see this! This is the most important photo shoot of my life!—"It doesn't matter"? Get the F*CK OUT of here!" Again, another example of people's feelings versus my logic. Where was the lie, though? Your most liked photo on Instagram won't receive as much attention as a mugshot of your arrest.

So, I made sure to pop a little smirk. If you take one lesson from Justin Bieber: smile in your mugshot. If you're going to be in that situation, the worst thing you can do is let people know that you're upset about being in jail. I don't know about you, but it makes me uncomfortable to see someone with a miserable expression on their face. Nobody is going to feel sorry for you anyway, so why give them those optics?

Since I was still high on meth, it absolutely didn't sink in to me how much trouble I was in. I had no clue that this was the end of the world as I had been living it. This was everything I dreaded, the worst possible end to my little love affair with meth. Up to this point, it was a secret. But still, the gravity of the situation—that everyone was going to find out about my meth use—didn't hit me. Since I was still feeling the high, I couldn't eat anything. I got to give away all my food, which made me feel like not such a scumbag for a minute.

My parents still think it was an act of God that I asked the cops to get my Beats bag with the drugs. They felt like God wanted me to get arrested so I could get caught, and they could help me stop using drugs. I don't think that theory conflicts with my reasoning; they could very well both be true. If I hadn't gotten caught, I don't see what the end point would have been. Remember, I still couldn't lift weights from my surgery. And I was having so much fun, I wasn't just going to wake up one day and say, "Let me put down the meth and get fat again." Somehow I thought meth was helping me avoid a backward slide in life.

Rehab, Winter 2017

I didn't think this would happen. I thought I was just having fun and doing what most other twenty-somethings were doing. It's such a gray area between fun and novelty to serious issue that it's hard to know when that line has been crossed. But if I had to pinpoint a moment, it would be sometime in December, when I looked in the mirror and noticed that my eyes were starting to get that "meth" look: the look I'd seen on some guys I met in Austin who had been doing ice for years; you know, where it wrinkles the skin around your eyes, and makes you look tired. My face has always been my best feature, *especially* my eyes. But when I saw that I might be doing permanent cosmetic damage to my face, I didn't even think about stopping. To me, that's the moment when I had officially gone beyond what I could handle.

To my surprise, one of the guards came and got me the next morning and told me I was being released. My initial excitement didn't last long because I knew I was about to have to face my parents. As I thought about what might be waiting for me outside, I almost didn't want to leave jail.

Their disappointment and sorrow had turned to scathing anger. I tried to tell them it was no big deal, and I genuinely thought that was the truth. I'm not sure I realized either how serious the charges were and how screwed I would be for the rest of my life if I were convicted of a drug felony.

As you probably know, parents blow drug use way out of proportion, and drug users try to downplay it.

My parents were no different. My mom started hysterically asking if I was going to be suffering through withdrawals; I'm not sure what a meth withdrawal even looks like, and I'm glad I never had to find out. The most withdrawal I ever suffered was going to 7-Eleven and eating a pint of ice cream. But I guess they weren't wrong in believing I was a hardcore drug user: when you're doing meth every day, that's hardcore baby.

My Uncle Shane and Aunt May were visiting us when I got out of jail. Neither of them had ever particularly liked me, so in the wake of my latest debacle, they were kind of the worst possible guests to have over. I thought, I can either say nothing to them and allow the tension to run rampant, or I can kill them with kindness. I saw an opportunity for a great bonding moment with my uncle, who used to have a problem with weed. I went up to him and said, "So I know you've had your problems in the past—is there anything I should know that you could tell me?"

My uncle probably never thought I would ask him for advice. "Wow," he said. Then he thought for a moment and added, "Be careful what you play with." He told me that he never thought he had a problem either, and then one day he wound up in Lewiston, Maine with a gun pointed in his face.

The decision was made for me to enter a thirty-day treatment center. My parents were consulting with the parents of a childhood friend of mine, who had been a serious heroin user, but was now doing well and no longer using. I told them sending me to rehab was ridiculous because I hadn't done meth in the past few days, and I was sitting there in front of them, perfectly fine! I wasn't detoxing, I wasn't going through violent withdrawals. I tried to convince them (and maybe myself a little) that I didn't have a drug problem. They were having none of it; the next day they would take me there. It was not optional.

Sure enough, we packed my stuff and drove up to the rehab place in New Hampshire.

I figured I had been through worse than thirty days in rehab. When I'd talked on the phone to a counselor there, he assured me the place wouldn't feel like a punishment. He said the food was really good, and that the place was co-ed, so I wasn't mad about it.

At first, I didn't get along with the people there. Wild, right? (Note: see every place I've ever been.)

This was a treatment center for extreme addicts. There was no one there who'd spent less than ten years using. Many of them were at the point where if they didn't stop, they were going to die. This was an end-of-the-line, last resort intervention for them. On the phone I had specifically expressed that I was worried the program would be too intense for someone at my stage of drug use. I was assured that it wouldn't.

Up until this point, I had been mostly full of sh*t trying to downplay my problem, but here's where I was right: I was in the opposite situation of everyone else there. They were at the final stage, while I was at the first stage. I had a hard time relating to what they were going through and they mostly thought it was a joke that I was there. Needless to say my first week in rehab was pretty rocky.

We went to AA meetings three times a week. If you've ever been to AA, you know it can be a very rigid atmosphere, and they take it very seriously. I didn't know that the etiquette at AA is very specific: you're not supposed to ask questions. I thought it was like a Q&A where we'd have a discussion.

After a few people had told their stories, I raised my hand and asked what I thought was a great question: "How do you deal with it when all the memories hit you, of the good times you had with your drug of choice—and you miss those times and want to go back?"

It was a legitimate question; this was me trying to take things seriously! If I was going to stop using meth then this was something I wanted help with. Unfortunately, I got in all kinds of trouble for asking a question. I was told not to open my mouth next time.

They were also pissed that it seemed like I was making light of my drug use. I wasn't talking about it in a soft and delicate tone, like a professional actor reading a dramatic monologue. You know that thing people will do, when they sit there for five minutes with an intense look on their face, trying to summon the words to say? I don't have that side to me. If I tried to get all melodramatic like that I would feel like a phony.

I was asking a genuine question, but I was trying to lighten the mood with my tone. Why did everyone there have to be so serious, every minute of every day? Whatever situation I find myself in, I always have this strong need to be the contrarian. If it's a tense atmosphere, I want to lighten the mood. If it's a light-hearted atmosphere, I want to make things tense. It's this insatiable urge I have to go against the grain. It was no different from when I was in second grade and my teacher would kick a kid's chair in anger; everyone else would be scared, and I would be laughing hysterically. You might be surprised to learn that being the person who always tries to subvert things doesn't always win friends and influence people!

For the first week of rehab, I was very unpopular. No one talked to me. What else is new? I had been unpopular and ignored so many times, it was impossible to count. If anyone there had read *Chasing the Rabbit*, they would have known that being unpopular and made to feel worthless and invisible was basically a way of life for me throughout most of my childhood.

It's quite a conflicted existence: wanting to always flip things upside down but also craving social approval and acceptance. At rehab, like the rest of my life, I kept trying to change people's opinions of me. Sometimes I win people over; sometimes I don't, but I always try. Much of my life I have noticed that the people who dislike me at first end up liking me in the long run, but the people who like me at first, end up disliking me. I think this is because my first impressions are misleading. So the dynamic you get is that the people who *like* what they initially see end up being wrong, and the people who *don't like* what they initially see end up being wrong. In other words, there was still time here at rehab!

I kept trying to be part of conversations, which has always been a struggle for me. I honestly don't know how you neurotypicals just naturally find yourselves inside these big group conversations, but I've always been able to distinguish the feeling of when you're truly part of one versus when you're trying to break in. It usually takes someone with high social value to bring me in and kind of instate me. Whatever skills you need to break into a conversation that's already happening, I don't have them.

About ten days into rehab, there was a turning point. There was a woman there named Deanna who reminded me of one of the chicks on *Jersey Shore*, except she was in her forties—so maybe like Snooki's mom. Deanna was very bubbly and outgoing, with a loud "New Joisey" accent. She was the first person who took to me, and she started including me in conversations.

On the second Sunday night, we were hanging out in the lounge. My sister had given me a *Pop Music Trivia* game for Christmas, and she sent it to me at rehab, hoping it would help me make some friends there. I put the game out on the table and acted like it wasn't mine. "Whose is this?" I asked. "You guys want to play?" 😉

Everyone was bored reading old magazines because there was no TV, so they agreed to play. Of course, I am (as Lance Bass used to call me) "the pop music encyclopedia." The questions seemed obscure to everyone but me.

I was almost worried they might think I was cheating! For example, someone read a card that said, "This album holds the record for most Top Five Billboard singles. Is it . . ." and there were multiple choices, but I didn't even need the choices—I just called out, "*Janet Jackson's Rhythm Nation 1814!*"

As useless as my music knowledge may be, in the right context it can be pretty attention-grabbing. After that game, all eyes were on me. Suddenly it was like I had a seat at the table. Once people give me a chance, talk to me and take the time to get to know me, that's all I need—I can take the ball and run with it. The problem I have is almost one of logistics. As I said, the people who give me a chance based on my first impression, end up not liking me, while the people who *would* end up liking me, often *don't* give me a chance based on my first impression—if that makes sense.

Later that night, the conversation came up of me having been in jail in three different states. I started telling the story of when I got arrested in Florida, trying to cop a knockoff brand Polo shirt (with the big pony). I had the whole room cracking up, and then someone asked, "What happened the next time?" And I told the story of getting arrested for making a joke bomb threat in Utah (there's a bonus chapter on that available on BadChoicesMake-GoodStories.com). It kept getting funnier and funnier, and then it was, "What happened the third time?" and I said "Oh, it's ridiculous . . . I accidently hit this girl with my car, and she thought I did it on purpose!" At that point I had basically turned the lounge into my own talk show.

That night, I made friends with the two most popular guys there; before that, they hadn't given me the time of day. From that point, rehab was another déjà vu of the Disney cruise ten years before. Once again, I was either the least popular guy, like at that boarding school in New Hampshire, or I was the top person there, like on the Disney cruise. Rarely do I find myself "sort of popular." That's because I don't just blend in: I'm either the center of attention or I get no attention. It's very unusual because most people's place on the social totem pole is generally static throughout their life, whereas mine is like a bipolar seesaw. Brendan, one of the popular guys there, actually remarked to me, "Dude, you had a meteoric rise—you literally went from being one of the bottom ten people to the number one person here."

But I can tell you, if I had been there a few years earlier when I was less mature, I probably would have been kicked out of that place at some point. This was a small, privately owned rehab facility, and they explained to us, "This is a two-way street: not only do you have to want to be here, but we have to want you here." Thank God by 2017 I was mature enough to hear that warning, look at my long history of being booted out of places, and recognize how easily this could be added to the list. I might not have had that foresight even a year before.

The last three weeks in rehab were some of the most fun days I've ever had, if you can believe it. I wish that I could say it was as much fun as doing drugs, but to be perfectly honest, nothing is that fun.

There were some cute girls at rehab. After the group starting putting me on this pedestal as the funniest guy there, the same girls that didn't even notice me a week earlier were now seeking out conversations with me. I told them how I love cats—I even had pictures of my cats with me. One of the girls had some cat socks, and she asked me if I liked them and said she was wearing them for me! 😄 Well, she was actually a mom in her fifties, but still.

I had brought some promotional cards to rehab with me to advertise my radio show, *Ridin With Dielawn*. Everyone loved the cards, and they started calling hanging out with me in the lounge "Ridin with Dielawn." Sometimes at night when we would do wrap-ups, people would say "Ridin with Dielawn" was the highlight of their day! That feeling is better than money, maybe even better than meth—well, let's not get crazy. 😉

All jokes aside, having gone through life struggling to establish and maintain relationships with people, I am not ashamed to say that being popular matters to me. Some people may find that egotistical or superficial, but those people should ask themselves why. I hear people talk about how they struggled their whole lives financially ("I grew up poor, we could barely afford to put bread on the table"), and those same people will be the first to tell you that people are more important than money ("the best things in life are free"). And guess what? They're absolutely right. The way people describe their struggles growing up underprivileged is exactly how I've felt my whole life about having relationships. You didn't have anything handed to you? Well I didn't have any social skills handed to me. I worked for every friend I had, I grinded for every date I got. And believe me, I would have gladly traded my middle-class upbringing for a social circle of friends that cared about me. So excuse me for valuing popularity; I value people.

I'm still in touch with some of the guys from rehab, and anytime I'm back in Maine, I hope to see them. Whenever I'm down on myself, I think about what I pulled off in those couple of weeks in rehab; it was truly something incredible. Whenever I'm lamenting over the good times I had doing meth (like right now, as I write this), I juxtapose my experience in rehab with my experience on the Dirty Pop cruise. On paper, who would ever think that rehab would be ten times as fun as a free Caribbean cruise with Lance Bass? It was drugs that made the difference. I look at my time in rehab as God showing me what could happen when I stopped using drugs.

My boys from Rehab! April 2017

When I was about to leave, the manager of the rehab facility, who knew my life story from talking to my dad, said, "Congratulations, Dylan! This might be the first place you haven't gotten kicked out of!" I never went in to rehab expecting to be sad to leave!

However, I was wary about getting carried away because the pattern throughout my life has been that when something goes really great—a knock-it-out-of-the-park home run—it's once. Every time you try to go back for more, the planets never end up aligning again. There's *no* chance I would go back to rehab and relive those three weeks of being the most popular person there. It's like a music artist who comes out with a huge debut album, and then there's that sophomore slump. So my first stint in rehab was Alanis Morrissette's *Jagged Little Pill,* but if I relapsed and ended up back there again, it would most certainly be *Supposed Former Infatuation Junkie*—her follow-up album that nobody remembers. I'd hate to see what a follow-up stint in rehab would look like. It would erase everything that happened the first time around, so I have to stay off drugs if I want to keep it to that one time with the great memories.

There are still times I think about meth and the great times I had while using, but I try to remember what it leads to. Comedian Dan Levy has a joke: "Don't do meth—meth never ends with a good story. It's never like, 'I was doing meth, now I'm a millionaire!'"

CONCLUSION

If you take one thing from this book, (besides don't do meth)—don't ever hear clichés the same way again. The next time you hear someone repeat a phrase that has been said many times before, whether it's "Just be yourself" or "Men just want sex" or "There's no such thing as normal," challenge the person who said it. Ask them if they have ever taken a second to think through these ideas, or if they're just repeating what society has fed them.

It's not that I don't believe girls should be helped, but there are many, many people and places out there giving guidance to females, so I'm going to wrap this up with some advice for the guys.

I'm not claiming to have it all figured out, because I don't. But one thing I have figured out, is that there is power in self-advocacy. I'm very lucky that with my looks and with my disability being invisible, I've been able get by as far as attracting girls and creating a social life. But I'm not naïve enough to think there aren't millions of guys out there, especially ones on the autism spectrum, who aren't getting by. It's not an issue of entitlement, I don't believe anyone should be entitled to friends or entitled to a mate, but I do believe it should be possible. It should be something that can be earned, something that can be worked for. There's a consensus that relationships are more important than money, right? Well then, as a society, much like the way we talk about helping people get into "the middle class," we should see a moral imperative to provide a path for the socially unskilled among us to be able to attract a mate, and to have friends.

Today, if a young man on the spectrum is struggling to attract the opposite sex, what are his options? If he fails with women, he'll be mocked, and if he tries researching any actual advice on how to be better with women, he'll be mocked. What if I didn't have my looks going for me, or my disability wasn't invisible? What if I had made it to twenty-seven and still hadn't had my first kiss? I guarantee you that being starved of human affection is worse than poverty. So why do we as a society think that's okay to allow?

It's not just guys with disabilities. Since the sexual revolution, the majority of men out there are completely shut off from any companionship of the opposite sex. It's far more than you'd think, because it's not something men like to admit. If they do speak up, they're laughted at. They're told that it's easy and that they just need to "man up." In other words, we insult their masculinity to shame them back into silence. We cannot continue to deprive mass numbers of average men from one of the most basic things in life, and not expect negative, and in some cases, violent, repercussions such as school shootings.

Of course, the responsibility for how things are largely falls on us men because we haven't spoken up for ourselves. A lot of men don't like to complain. They feel like there's a stigma that goes with advocating for themselves, or criticizing the way they're being treated. They feel like if they have to complain, they're somehow less of a man. But you know what's really not manly? Losing. Let's face it, we men have gotten our asses kicked in the last fifty years. Until we get over the aversion we have to saying, "Hey, I deserve a chance," none of the things I just talked about will change. Nobody does this apply to more than individuals on the autism spectrum. Any solutions to the issues I just described will remain pipe dreams if we do not advocate for ourselves.

I am fortunate that I've never had a problem complaining, but even when I was so inappropriate that I was sent away to Asperger's boot camp in the wilderness, I still believed that I was worthy of friendship. I believed to my core that I was worthy of girls' attention. Don't let society tell you that you aren't good enough. Go out there and claim your spot. Between me and you, you might not be good enough, YET. But you can get there. If you had met me as a child, or even when I was fat in 2012, you would have never thought I could be the man you see today, so you can get there too. Don't let people treat you like you're disposable. If people are rejecting you, demand that they give you a reason why and then listen to their feedback. If someone isn't going to give you the chance you deserve, they can *at least* give you some constructive criticism.

I am now living in Los Angeles, pursuing my dream of becoming a media personality. I'm out here making connections and hustling my talents, and I hope to someday make a living being a talk show personality or maybe a reality show star. Don't you think a reality show based on my life would blow the Kardashians out of the water?

If you want to keep up with my daily opinions on things and funny videos I make, subscribe to my YouTube channel—"Real Dielawn." You can just go to YouTube.com/RealDielawn

And I also post daily videos on Facebook on my page "Real Dielawn."

And on Instagram @RealDielawn

And on Snapchat—RealDielawn

And my Twitter feed is pretty lit too @RealDielawn

Easy to remember right? 😜

Oh, and I also offer social skills coaching, go to BadChoices-MakeGoodStories.com for a free consultation.

Also if you bought this book through Amazon and enjoyed it, PLEASE consider writing a review for me, they are very important. Also, I read them all and would really like to know your thoughts! 👏

Acknowledgments

I wish to thank everyone who allowed me to use their real names, my father who helped me painstakingly comb through my life's stories, my mother for providing limitless moral support and helping me proofread (even though I undid most of her edits), my sisters who helped me pick out the photos, Daniel Yeager who stayed patient through my uncountable changes to the cover design, Jesse Lee Peterson and Doug Massey for helping me shoot the cover photos, and Grace Peirce and Karen Harrison for fantastic editing work!

About the Author

DYLAN "DIELAWN" VOLK: After years of what his parents called "the diagnosis of the month club," Dylan was diagnosed with High Functioning Autism at the age of eight. Life has been a minefield of obstacles for Dylan. When he was little, he struggled with learning the rules and following directions that did not make sense to him. As he got older, he was challenged, especially socially, by a world that seemed extremely confusing to him, with a disability that to most was invisible. Even today, Dylan works hard to figure out what he needs to do in order to get through each day as a twenty-seven-year-old adult with autism in our fast-paced and often unforgiving society.

Dylan graduated from Sedgefield High School in 2010 and is currently pursuing his goal of making it in the entertainment industry. He has a YouTube channel under his stage name "Real Dielawn" where viewers are treated on a daily basis to a look inside his one-of-a-kind mind. Dylan has also been a regular on SiriusXM's "Dirty Pop Live" hosted by Lance Bass, heard formerly on OutQ Channel 106 and RadioAndy Channel 102. He has hosted his own radio show, "Ridin with Dielawn" which aired Saturday nights in Portland, Maine, on WLOB 100.5-FM and via his podcast.

Dylan has been enjoying his experiences speaking about his life and the book he wrote with his father. His presentations to thousands of people from coast to coast have been overwhelmingly well-received. He hopes his work helping his father write *Chasing the Rabbit: A Dad's Life Raising a Son on the Autism Spectrum* and his new book, *Bad Choices Make Good Stories: My Life with Autism*, will help families as they navigate through the difficulties of living life on the spectrum. He currently resides in Los Angeles, CA.